How
Tea Cosies
Changed
the World

If you are cold, tea will warm you. If you are too heated, it will cool you.
If you are depressed, it will cheer you. If you are excited, it will calm you.

William Gladstone, 1865

For Mrs Olix Dax, aka Alexandra Daw, nee Conner, otherwise
known as Luvvie (because she is wont to call everyone else Luvvie),
The Fairy Queen (as in 'said the Fairy Queen', proudly announced
on the making of rude noises) and Fairy Godmother to everyone
and their children and their dogs. You are my cup of tea, Olix.

How Tea Cosies
Changed the World

Loani Prior

MURDOCH BOOKS

Contents

Egg Daisies

Beatrice

Starry Night

Graphs — 141

Arty stuff

So here we are again. Book three.

What moves those of genius, what inspires their work is not new ideas,
but their obsession with the idea that what has already been said is still not enough.
Eugene Delacroix

Mr Delacroix may have been talking about the art of the French Romantics and I'm no genius, but I reckon there is plenty still to say about the little old tea cosy. Some opinionated folk have suggested that I must be done now and what about a beanie book or, heaven forbid, toilet roll covers. One wouldn't suggest to an artist she had done enough portraits, and that she might move on to landscapes! Would one? Harrumph!

My publisher couldn't care less about MY not being done with tea cosies but it seems YOU are not done with them either. It is likely that you will never be done with them. We could end up with the Golden Hands Encyclopaedia of Tea Cosies. Now there's a thought.

The secret of the tea cosy

It was Joan that let me in on the secret of the tea cosy. I met Joan at the launch of the first book, *Wild Tea Cosies*, at the book-signing end of the evening. She handed me her copy and then pulled out her own tea cosy to show me.

It was old and more bare than threadbare but she held that tea cosy like it was her favourite thing in the world and she told me a story.

Joan's grandmother had knitted the tea cosy with her own young hands when she was a new bride. She had used it every day of her married life and when she died, Joan's mother had taken the cosy and used it too and now that she was dead, it was Joan's. That funny old thing was almost eighty years old and it was filled with all the love and memories of three lifetimes. A proper heirloom.

And that is the secret of the tea cosy.

That, and the fact that they are completely ridiculous. Even when they are not meant to be ridiculous, they are ridiculous. And funny. I already knew that bit deep down in my belly. You know, like babies are cute. How can you not love a cute baby, or a funny tea cosy? Oh alright, so there are some of you who don't love cute babies. But not many. A minuscule minority. Hardly worth mentioning. But everyone loves a tea cosy.

But is it art?

Anything can become an objet d'art, stuck in a glass cabinet with a label and some good downlighting. Even a tea cosy. And mine have been in such a place! But do I make art? I ask the question here only because I get asked that question myself, often. What can I say? A wild imagination tempered with that old counterpart, boundaries, helps to produce something in-tress-ting and I do enjoy a lustful passion for colour.

Divining design

Ideas are miraculous things. The more ideas you have, the more ideas you have.

I see tea cosies in everything. The most important thing about design is to be game. Game to get it wrong. To discard the flotsam and jetsam and concentrate on the jewels. I have a mountain of prototypes, design duds, bugger ups, all made without any disappointment, all leading me somewhere new. Good design wouldn't be good design without attention to form AND function. No point in having a tea cosy that looks wild but won't stand up by itself, is too heavy to lift or can't be washed. I follow the old rules, like three is better than two, off to the side is better than in the middle. But then, what is a rule if it isn't for breaking?

Sometimes 'less' is more and sometimes 'gloriously camp exuberance' is more. That is good advice to follow.

If I were to impart any gem at all, it might be that the difference between something artful and something Blue Rinse can be as inoffensive as a plastic bee. Be very afraid of the plastic bee I say, yes I do.

Ah! See what happens when you get to book three? One imagines One's advice might be highly sought after and One ought not to be stingy, and give it.

Remembering Grandma

None of that REALLY matters. What matters is that my wild and woolly tea warmers might just entice you to pick up your needles after twenty years. It matters that they make you smile. It matters that you might be game to try your own mad designs.

And it matters that they remind you of your grandmother.

Portraits of a tea cosy

After Joan brought that first cosy to show me, Tea Cosy Fetishists have been turning up in droves to have their portraits taken with their own favourite tea cosy. Yes they have. Young and not so young TCFs. Women AND men. Yes men! And dogs.

Mark Crocker photographed the first book, *Wild Tea Cosies*, and this year, in the year of Our Lord 2012, he and I are collecting portraits and tea cosy stories to add to our stash and to exhibit on the national stage in 2013. (Errr, that would be the Australian national stage.) When you see us in your town, be sure to come and say hello and get snapped for posterity, and for fun. You can tell a great deal about a person by their tea cosy, did you know? A great deal.

The technical bit

Knitting in the round

So! You haven't ever knitted in the round before? I can't recall ever knitting in the round myself, before starting all this tea cosy madness. Nup. Not for the life of me. Not one recollection. Now I want to knit everything in the round. Everything. It just seems very clever. I feel very clever knitting in the round, but then, I'm easily pleased.

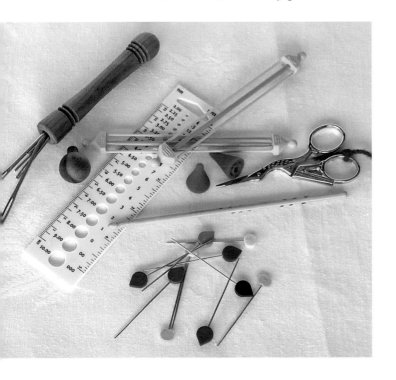

Knitting on the straight

I use circular needles for everything, even when knitting on the straight. It is so much easier to measure the fabric mid project. It is easier to try on. If it is a great big weighty thing I'm knitting, like a brown jumper, it rests easily on my lap. Straight needles are for the birds and for vintage collections and for sticking in your French Bun like scary old Mrs Frogmorton who lives above the corner store smoking foul-smelling cigars and shouting at little children from behind her stained lace curtains. Gawd! Where did that come from?

The patterns in this book

For each of the patterns knitted in the round, I have given MY preferred method for that particular job. Any method is valid.

Methods for knitting in the round

Double-pointed needles (dpns)

EQUIPMENT

6 double-pointed needles: 4 for holding the stitches, 1 for working the stitches and 1 for sticking in your dreadlocks. No dreadlocks or nose piercings? So make that 5 dpns.

GETTING STARTED

Cast on 8 stitches onto one dpn. Arrange the stitches evenly onto four needles. Join in the round (see page 13) and use the fifth needle to knit the stitches from Needle 1. Needle 1 then becomes the working needle, knitting the stitches from Needle 2, and so on.

One set of circular needles (magic loop)

EQUIPMENT

ONE set of circular needles with a long cable length — 80 cm (31½ in) from needle tip to needle tip will do the job nicely for a tea cosy knitted in the round using the Magic Loop.

GETTING STARTED

Cast on 8 stitches.
Count 4 stitches and pull the cable out into a loop between the fourth and fifth stitches. Join in the round.
Knit half the round, then set up the loops and cables ready to knit the other half round. You need one needlepoint to knit from (holding the stitches) and one needlepoint to knit with (free of stitches). As you increase the stitches, always keep the cable looped at each halfway mark.

Two sets of circular needles

Cat Bordhi devised this method of knitting in the round. Whenever I am unsure of the best way to do anything, the very first thing I do is Google Cat Bordhi on YouTube. Cat is the Queen of Clever Techniques.

EQUIPMENT

TWO sets of circular needles. Funny that! Perhaps that should read two SETS of circular needles. Yes they should be the same needle diameter and the same cable length — 60 cm (24 in) from needle tip to needle tip will do nicely for tea cosies.

GETTING STARTED

Cast on 8 stitches.
Slip 4 stitches onto the other SET of circular needles. Join in the round (see opposite). Always knit half of the stitches with one SET of circular needles and the other half with the OTHER set of circular needles.

When it is time to change needle sets, slip the stitches you have just completed down onto the flexible cable section. Ignore these stitches and this set of needles. Pretend those stitches are sitting there on a stitch holder. They are done with, until the next time round. Pick up the other set of needles and prepare the first stitches by slipping them up off the

flexible cable and onto the needle to meet the working yarn. Find the other needle end of THAT SET to use as your working needle.

Joining in the round

Remember, you are knitting in the ROUND. Around and around, not back and forth as you do when you are knitting ROWS. Check that the cast-on stitches are not twisted. Join the last cast-on stitch you made to the first cast-on stitch you made, simply by knitting the first cast-on stitch. If you have used the double or long tail cast-on method (see page 14), you will make a firm join by using the working thread AND the tail together as a double thread. Just knit the FIRST stitch with the double thread, then drop the tail. When you come back to it, remember, this is ONE stitch with a double thread, not two single stitches.

I now much prefer this method of joining than the one described in *REALLY Wild Tea Cosies*. It is less fussy than making an extra stitch. And firmer.

Avoiding extra stitches

The most common mistake when knitting in the round is to add a stitch at the change over of needles, in all methods. Take your time to arrange the working thread so that it is not wrapped around needles or cables.

Other stuff

Double or long tail cast-on

Cast on using the Double or Long Tail method. That way, you will have the tail and the working thread together at the same place — at the last stitch. If you don't know the long tail method and are keen to learn, look up your knitting bible, or Google YouTube 'double cast-on' or 'long tail cast-on'. It isn't absolutely necessary to use this method but …

Jeny's surprisingly elastic bind-off

Try Jeny Staiman's Surprisingly Elastic Bind-Off. This method of casting off is not invisible. It creates a nice edging as well as a loose cast-off. It is not for every occasion. It is easy AND surprisingly elastic! It goes like this:

Knit the first stitch, yarn over knitwise, knit the next stitch, scoop the back two stitches over the front stitch and off the working needle, yarn over knitwise again, knit the next stitch, scoop the back two stitches up over the front stitch, and so on.

If you are casting off in a ribbed pattern, take the yarn over purlwise and purl the next stitch before scooping the back two stitches over the front stitch. If you are unsure, and you are a modern woman, Google Jeny's Surprisingly Elastic Bind-Off

for the YouTube video. Gees I love the web. And I love all the clever generous women sharing their knitting nous with the world.

Mattress stitch

Mattress stitch is a beaut way to sew up two pieces of knitted fabric. The stitches are hidden and the seam is seamless. Lay the two edges side by side with the right side facing you. Thread a darning needle with

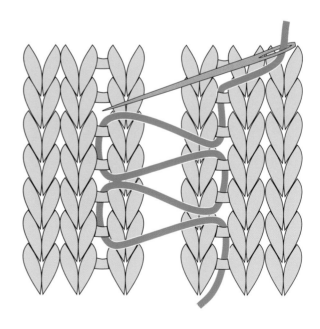

yarn that matches the edges you are joining. Working from bottom to top, pick up the first stitch (adjacent to the cast-off) on the right-hand edge, and then pick up the first stitch (adjacent to the cast-off) on the left-hand edge. Continue working right edge, left edge, four or five times, and then pull the thread tight, drawing the edges together. The seam will magically disappear. Continue to the end of the seam in this manner.

Blanket stitch

Every knitter should know how to do blanket stitch — so refresh your memory. You could go scurrying off to find diagrams of blanket stitch or you could look at this one, to save time. You just never know when you will need it.

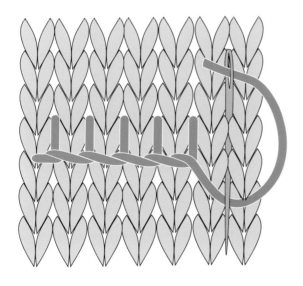

M1 — or make one or make 1 or maaake oooonnnne

To M1 is to increase by lifting up the connecting thread between the stitch you have just worked and the stitch you are about to work, onto the left (waiting) needle. Knit into the back of it and slip it off. Careful though. You want to make an extra stitch without making a lace hole. It has to do with the way you place that thread up on the waiting needle. But you'll be able to work that bit out — just by knowing that you want to make an extra stitch without making a lace hole.

Only some of the answers

My little book is not meant to be a teacher of knitting techniques, so if anything is not explained as well as you'd like, please take the time to look up other books or search the web. YouTube has some great teaching videos about every conceivable knitting and crochet technique. I have learned a great deal online. And if you don't already have one, invest in a knitting bible. There are some excellent books on the market, old and new. I wouldn't be without mine.

The Basic Tea Cosy

{KNITTED TEA COSY}

*Teapots come in all shapes and sizes and my patterns might
not fit your pot exactly. You could always make the cosy and find
the pot to fit, but your favourite teapot will stay there all cold and
naked. Not a pretty sight or a happy situation for a teapot to be in.*

*By working in the ROUND from the TOP DOWN, or from
the CENTRE OUT, it is easy to measure the size of the cosy to the size
of the teapot as you go AND you can design your own beanies and berets
and bags and cushion covers and space ships and measure to size as you go.*

*It is also easy to shape the circle into a short or tall cone,
depending on the number of rounds you work between each increasing
or decreasing round. There is soooo much fun to be had with a circle.*

*Throughout the book, you will be referred back to the
Basic Tea Cosy to make a body or a lining. Needle sizes and
yarn weights are listed in each individual pattern.*

So here it is, the Basic Tea Cosy.

Size

To fit a six-cup teapot that stands 13 cm (5 in)
tall (not including the knob) and 12 cm (4¾ in) in
diameter (not including the spout and handle).

Method

Knitted in the ROUND from the top
down. Sides are knitted in ROWS.

Round 8: *K3, increase in next stitch, repeat from * to end of round.

Round 10: *K4, increase in next stitch, repeat from * to end of round.

Continue in this increasing pattern until there are 10 stitches in each segment of the pie (80 sts).

OR STOP the increasing pattern earlier, when the diameter of the circle is big enough for the teapot you are using. This might be FEWER than a total of 80 stitches. Be sure to measure against the teapot well before then.

Knit one round without shaping.
(**Wood Fungus and Eugenie only:** Purl one round.)

SIDES

Worked in ROWS (not rounds).
Begin working the first side with the right side facing.

Note. If you are using the Magic Loop method (see page 11) to make the Basic Tea Cosy, you will have to slip half the stitches onto a stitch holder while you work down one side.

Another Note. If you are using the TWO SETS of circular needles method (see page 12), then one set of cables becomes the stitch holder. Beaut huh!?

*Yet Another Note. The following ribbed pattern is a K1, P1 rib, but in some patterns I have used a K2, P2 rib for the outer body. Simply replace [*K1, P1, repeat from * to end of row] with [*K2, P2, repeat from * to end of row]. The pink cosy pictured opposite shows K2, P2 rib.*

Body/body lining

UPPER BODY

Using the needles and yarn specified in your pattern, cast on 8 stitches.
Join in the round.

Round 1 (and each alternate round): Knit.

Round 2: Increase by knitting into the front and back of each stitch.

Round 4: *K1, increase in next stitch, repeat from * to end of round.

Round 6: *K2, increase in next stitch, repeat from * to end of round.

Row 1: Knit.
Row 2: *K1, P1, repeat from * to end of row.
Row 3: *K1, P1, repeat from * to end of row.
Repeat rows 2 and 3 until the ribbed side measures long enough to cover the bowl of the teapot.
Cast off using Jeny's Surprisingly Elastic Bind-Off (see page 14).

Work the second Side the same.

Putting it all together

Sew the sides together using mattress stitch (see page 14) on each of the Bodies below the spout and handle. Turn the shorter lining (see The Last Note, below) inside out and place inside the Outer Body. The wrong sides of the Body and the Body Lining should be facing each other. Secure the Body Lining to the Outer Body by loosely stitching around the handle and spout openings with a simple tacking stitch.

The Last Note. Make the Body Lining slightly shorter in the sides (just a row or two) than the Outer Body so that it doesn't poke out like an unruly petticoat.

Wood Fungus

{KNITTED TEA COSY}

For Maria of Moss Vale

*What a star you are, Maria! Honestly, whenever there is someone in my
knitting workshop who worries too much about their ability to knit
well enough, or to learn fast enough, I want you there to show them how.
Not to show them how to knit well enough or to learn fast enough,
but to show them how to value the gift of having a go without fear.
And what a lesson! Maria, you are blind and you not only knit,
but you knit beautifully. Wood Fungus is yours to touch, now
that it has been photographed for the sighted masses.*

Size

To fit a six-cup teapot that stands 13 cm (5 in)
tall (not including the knob) and 12 cm (4¾ in) in
diameter (not including the spout and handle).

Materials

* 2 x 50 g (1¾ oz) balls Noro Kureyon
  wool, Main Colour (MC)
* 1 x 50 g (1¾ oz) ball Nundle Collection
  8-ply wool, Contrast Colour (CC)

Equipment

* Two sets 4 mm (UK 8, USA 6)
  circular needles, 60 cm (24 in) long
  from needle tip to needle tip
* Darning needle
* Scissors
* Polyester fibrefill

Method

Knitted in the ROUND from the top down. I prefer to use TWO SETS of circular needles for this job (see page 12).

Mushrooms (knitted in one piece)

Using both sets of 4 mm (UK 8, USA 6) circular needles and MC, cast on 8 stitches. Join in the round.

TOPSIDE OF 1ST (SMALLEST) MUSHROOM

Round 1 (and each alternate round): Knit.
Round 2: Increase by knitting into the front and back of each stitch.
Round 4: *K1, increase in next stitch, repeat from * to end of round.
Round 6: *K2, increase in next stitch, repeat from * to end of round.
Round 8: *K3, increase in next stitch, repeat from * to end of round.
Round 10: *K4, increase in next stitch, repeat from * to end of round.
Round 11: Knit.

Note. There are 8 segments to the pie, each now with 6 stitches — a total of 48 stitches around.

Round 12: Purl (this creates a nice folding line at the edge of the mushroom head).

UNDERSIDE OF 1ST MUSHROOM

Change to CC.
Round 1: *K4, K2tog, repeat from * to end of round.
Round 2 (and each alternate round): Knit.
Round 3: *K3, K2tog, repeat from * to end of round.

Round 5: *K2, K2tog, repeat from * to end of round.
Round 7: *K1, K2tog, repeat from * to end of round.
Round 8: Knit.

Note. There are 8 segments to the pie, each now with 2 stitches — a total of 16 stitches around.

TOPSIDE OF 2ND MUSHROOM

Change to MC.
Round 1: *K1, increase in next stitch, repeat from * to end of round.
Round 2 (and each alternate round): Knit.
Round 3: *K2, increase in next stitch, repeat from * to end of round.
Round 5: *K3, increase in next stitch, repeat from * to end of round.
Continue in this increasing pattern, until there are 7 stitches in each segment of the pie — a total of 56 stitches around.
Round 13: Knit.
Round 14: Purl.

UNDERSIDE OF 2ND MUSHROOM

Change to CC.
Round 1: *K5, K2tog, repeat from * to end of round.
Round 2 (and each alternate round): Knit.
Round 3: *K4, K2tog, repeat from * to end of round.
Continue in this decreasing pattern, until there are 2 stitches in each segment of the pie — a total of 16 stitches.

TOPSIDE OF 3RD MUSHROOM

Change to MC.
Begin as for Topside of 2nd Mushroom.
Continue in this increasing pattern until there are 8 stitches in each segment of the pie — a total of 64 stitches around.
Round 15: Knit.
Round 16: Purl.

UNDERSIDE OF 3RD MUSHROOM

Change to CC.
Round 1: *K6, K2tog, repeat from * to end of round.
Round 2 (and each alternate round): Knit.
Round 3: *K5, K2tog, repeat from * to end of round.
Continue in this decreasing pattern until there are 2 stitches in each segment of the pie — a total of 16 stitches.

TOPSIDE OF 4TH MUSHROOM

Change to MC.
Begin as for Topside of 2nd Mushroom.
Continue in this increasing pattern until there are 9 stitches in each segment of the pie — a total of 72 stitches around.
Round 17: Knit.
Round 18: Purl.

UNDERSIDE OF 4TH MUSHROOM

Change to CC.
Round 1: *K7, K2tog, repeat from * to end of round.
Round 2 (and each alternate round): Knit.

there are 10 stitches in each segment of the pie — a total of 80 stitches around. And here endeth your lessen in the eight times table.
Round 19: Knit.
Round 20: Purl.

UNDERSIDE OF 5TH MUSHROOM

Change to CC.
Round 1: *K8, K2tog, repeat from * to end of round.
Round 2 (and each alternate round): Knit.
Round 3: *K7, K2tog, repeat from * to end of round.
Continue in this decreasing pattern until there are 2 stitches in each segment of the pie — a total of 16 stitches.
Cast off loosely.

Body (make 2)

Worked in ROUNDS from the top down.
  You will make 2 Bodies, one in the main colour and one to place inside as a lining. A lining makes the cosy warm but, more importantly, it gives the Body the strength to carry the mushroom top. It is, after all, a little knitted sculpture.

Using both sets of 4 mm (UK 8, USA 6) circular needles and MC, cast on 8 stitches. Join in the round.
  Proceed as for the **Basic Tea Cosy** (see page 16), remembering to purl that extra round at the edge of the top, as mentioned in the pattern.

Round 3: *K6, K2tog, repeat from * to end of round.
Continue in this decreasing pattern until there are 2 stitches in each segment of the pie — a total of 16 stitches.

TOPSIDE OF 5TH MUSHROOM

Change to MC.
Begin as for Topside of 2nd Mushroom.
Continue in this increasing pattern until

Putting it all together

Stuff each of the mushrooms with the fibrefill, but not too tightly. Be sure to spread the stuffing evenly and right out into the edges of the mushroom. Yes, there is only a small hole at the bottom of a 5-tiered sculpture but it is possible. Take the time to fill and spread to get a really lovely shape to each mushroom. Sit the mushroom contraption on the body of the teapot and play with the fall of the concertina sections. When you have decided how it should sit, secure the middle mushrooms to each other and then the whole thing to the Body with some secret and well-placed stitches.

Le Grand Couvre-théière

{KNITTED TEA COSY WITH MAGIC WEAVING AND SOME SEWING}

For Merryn

*How is it that Merryn gets mentioned in all three tea cosy books?,
I hear you ask. Well, the story is less about Merryn and more about
never saying never, as in 'I would never use that yarn in a million years'.*

*Merryn carried around 4 little balls of Manx Loaghtan wool all over
Europe in 2006, bought from her hometown in the Isle of Man pour moi
(gees, my French is good isn't it). When she gave me that little present,
I couldn't ever imagine using it. It just isn't very pretty, or soft.*

*But one ought never say never, 'cos here we are at book three, having used
it so fabulously in book one and in book two, and now in book three, we
(that is the royal 'we', as in Queen of the Tea Cosies 'we') are using it
THREE TIMES IN ONE BOOK. Zeez tea cozee ecz for you Merryn. Big time.*

Size

The teapot can be any size at all. The
cosy stands 22 cm (8½ in) tall to the rim
and is 33 cm (13 in) across the horizontal
edge. She is BIG and beautiful!

Materials

OUTER COSY (KNITTED)
* 2 x 50 g (1¾ oz) balls Heirloom
  Naturals Manx Loaghtan 8-ply wool

* 1 x 50 g (1¾ oz) ball Nundle
  Collection 8-ply wool: Amethyst
* 1 x 50 g (1¾ oz) ball Debbie Bliss
  Donegal Luxury Tweed Aran (First
  weaving thread): Lavender
* 1 x 50 g (1¾ oz) ball Patons Luxury
  Mohair (Second weaving thread): Purple
* 24 little felted balls (12 for each side)

COSY LINING (SEWN)

* 80 x 80 cm (31½ x 31½ in) cotton print fabric
* 80 x 80 cm (31½ x 31½ in) iron-on stiff interfacing
* Sewing needle and cotton thread to match cotton print fabric
* Large piece of paper (newspaper will do), for template

Equipment

* One set 5 mm (UK 6, USA 8) circular needles, 80 cm (31½ in) long from needle tip to needle tip
* Two sets 4 mm (UK 8, USA 6) circular needles, 80 cm (31½ in) long from needle tip to needle tip

* 3 mm (UK 11, USA C) crochet hook for weaving
* Darning needle
* Scissors
* Pins

Method

Sides knitted on the straight. I used ONE SET of circular needles. Yes, to knit on the straight. Rim knitted in the round. I used TWO SETS of circular needles (see page 12).

FIRST THINGS FIRST

Sometimes the order in which you make the parts greatly affects the sum of those parts. This is one of those times.

1 Knit both Sides.
2 Weave in the pretty colours.
3 Block both Sides. Definitely block the Sides.
4 Knit the Gusset to the length of the outside arc.
5 Make the paper template for the lining.
6 Cut and sew the lining.
7 Join the knitted Sides to the knitted Gusset.
8 Pick up stitches around the opening and knit a rolled rim.
9 Insert the cotton lining into the knitted cosy and stitch it all together.

Sides (make 2)

I'm going to start you off in the conventional manner with written instructions for the first few rows but then, when you are into the swing of things, it will be much easier to refer to the graph (on page 152). So! You have never read a pattern from a graph before? Gorn! It is easy. If I can draw a graph, you can read it.

Working in ROWS and using 5 mm (UK 6, USA 8) needles and Lavender Donegal Tweed Aran, cast on 8 stitches. (That is 2 stitches for each end of the semi circle and 4 for the repeating increasing pattern.)

Row 1 (and each alternate row — wrong side): Purl.
Row 2: K2, *increase in the next stitch by knitting into the front and back of it, repeat from * to the last 2 stitches, K2.
Row 4: K2, *K1, increase in the next stitch, repeat from * to the last 2 stitches, K2.

There is now a change in the way you increase. Instead of knitting into the front and back of a stitch, you will now Make 1 (M1) — see page 15.

Row 6: K2, *K1, M1, K1, M1, K1, repeat from * to the last 2 stitches, K2.
Row 7 (and each alternate row): Purl.
Row 8: Knit.
Row 10: K2, *K2, M1, K1, M1, K2, repeat from * to the last 2 stitches, K2.
Row 12: Knit.
Row 14: K2, *K3, M1, K1, M1, K3, repeat from * to the last 2 stitches, K2.

Cut Lavender yarn and join in Manx Loaghtan yarn.

Row 16: Knit.
Row 18: K2, *K4, M1, K1, M1, K4, repeat from * to the last 2 stitches, K2.
Row 20: Knit.
STOP! Don't purl the next row. The instructions change now.

Go to Le Grand Sac à Main pattern (on page 152) and, reading from the GRAPH,

continue on from Row 15. Yes, Row 15. Check the legend explaining the graph. In case you have never read from a graph before, I will get you started with the written pattern, as follows:

Row 15 of Graph: P2, *K4, P3, K4, repeat from * to last 2 stitches, P2.
Row 16 of Graph: K2, *P4, M1, K1, M1, P4, repeat from * to last 2 stitches, K2.

Row 17 of Graph: P2, *K4, P5, K4, repeat from * to last 2 stitches, P2.
Row 18 of Graph: K2, *P4, K5, P4, repeat from * to last 2 stitches, K2.
Row 19 of Graph: P2, *K4, P5, K4, repeat from * to last 2 stitches, P2.
Row 20 of Graph: K2, *P4, K1, M1, K1, M1, K1, P4, repeat from * to last 2 stitches, K2.
Row 21 of Graph: P2, *K4, P7, K4, repeat from * to last 2 stitches, P2.
Row 22 of Graph: K2, *P4, K7, P4, repeat from * to last 2 stitches, K2.

Look at your knitting. Look at the graph. Look at the written instructions above. See how they all match. Don't be shy. Off you go and follow the graph. Remember that you must always work 2 stitches at the beginning of the row, then knit the repeating pattern of the graph, and work 2 stitches at the end of the row. This will give you seams to work with when putting it all together.

CASTING OFF

Use Jeny's Surprising Elastic Bind-Off (see page 14).

Weaving and other stuff

Now turn over to the instructions for Le Grand Sac à Main (on page 35), because you need to follow the directions for Weaving (using Lavender Tweed Aran and Purple Luxury Mohair in place of the Cerise wool and Powdery Pink Mohair), Blocking,

knitting the Gusset (using Amethyst yarn in place of Cerise), making a Paper Template, sewing a Cotton Lining and constructing the Knitted Outer Bag. When you've done all that, come back here for the Knitted Rim.

Knitted rim

Using two sets of 4 mm (UK 8, USA 6) needles and Amethyst yarn, with the right side facing you, pick up about 90 stitches along one Side, then 8 stitches across where the Gusset meets the opening of the cosy, another 90 stitches along the other Side and another 8 stitches at the other end of the Gusset.

Purl for 8 rounds.

Cast off with Jeny's Surprisingly Elastic Bind-Off (see page 14).

Putting it all together

Insert the lining into the knitted bag. Pin the rolled (reverse stocking stitch) rim to the very bottom of the lining edge closing up the roll as you go. Using the cotton thread and the sewing needle, stitch the rolled rim to the bottom of the lining with small and secret stitches.

Using the photograph as a guide, sew the little felted balls between the woven rectangles — 12 balls per Side.

Le Grand Sac à Main

{KNITTED BAG WITH MAGIC WEAVING AND SOME SEWING}

That is French for Big Bag.

I thought of myself as Lady Loani of Noosa, living in a stately home with nothing better to do than while away the hours knitting and weaving and sewing … for hours on end, with pretty threads and cloth in front of me, stitching up la grande bourse. That is French for 'big purse'.

'Tis a wordy way of saying The Bag takes a long time. Settle in. TAKE your time. Enjoy the knitting. Savour the weaving and make free a Sunday of hours to measure and cut and sew the lining. It will all be worth it.

Size

She stands 22 cm (8½ in) tall to the rim and is 33 cm (13 in) across the horizontal edge.

Materials

Note. It is not essential to use the specified yarns for the weaving part of the project. Choose a vibrant contrasting colour to the muddy Manx Loaghtan, and something in the same weight or less. Wait until you have knitted, woven and blocked the Sides before shopping for the cane handles.

OUTER BAG (KNITTED)

* 2 x 50 g (1¾ oz) balls Heirloom Naturals Manx Loaghtan 8-ply wool
* 2 x 50 g (1¾ oz) balls Nundle Collection 8-ply wool (First weaving thread): Cerise
* 1 x 25 g (⅞ oz) ball Sublime kid mohair blend (Second weaving thread): Soft Powdery Pink
* Cane handles (see Note opposite)
* Large button or felted ball, for catch

BAG LINING (SEWN)

* 80 x 80 cm (31½ x 31½ in) cotton print fabric
* 80 x 80 cm (31½ x 31½ in) iron-on stiff interfacing
* Cotton thread to match cotton print fabric
* Large piece of paper (newspaper will do), for template

Equipment

* One set 5 mm (UK 6, USA 8)
  circular needles, 80 cm (31½ in) long
  from needle tip to needle tip
* One set 4 mm (UK 8, USA 6)
  circular needles, 80 cm (31½ in) long
  from needle tip to needle tip
* 3 mm (UK 11, USA C) crochet
  hook for weaving
* Darning needle
* Sewing needle
* Scissors
* Pins

Method

Sides knitted on the STRAIGHT
with ONE SET of circular needles.
Rim knitted on the STRAIGHT
with ONE SET of circular needles.
Circular needles knit around bends
better. They do. They do.

FIRST THINGS FIRST

Sometimes the order in which you make
the parts greatly affects the sum of those
parts. This is one of those times.

1   Knit both Sides.
2   Weave in the pretty colours.
3   Block both Sides. Definitely
    block the Sides.
4   Knit the Gusset to the length
    of the outside arc. (Now you
    can buy the handles.)
5   Make the paper template for the lining.

6   Cut and sew the lining.
7   Join the knitted Sides to the knitted Gusset.
8   Pick up stitches around the opening
    and knit a rolled rim.
9   Insert the cotton lining into the
    knitted bag and stitch it all together.
10   Add handles and the catch.

Sides (make 2)

I'm going to start you off in the conventional
manner with written instructions for the first
few rows but then, when you are into the swing
of things, it will be much easier to refer to the
graph. Don't go all funny. It's just a graph.

Working in ROWS and using 5 mm
(UK 6, USA 8) needles and Manx
Loaghtan yarn, cast on 32 stitches.

Row 1 (wrong side): Knit.
Row 2: Purl.
Work a further 7 rows in stocking
stitch, ending with a knit row.
This makes the roll-up collar that will
hold the cane handles in place.
The reverse (purl) side of the stocking
stitch should now be facing you. This is
the RIGHT side of the knitted fabric.
Mark the right side of the knitted fabric
with a little tie of contrasting coloured wool.

Row 10 (right side): K2, *K2, increase
by knitting into the front and back of the
next stitch, K1, increase by knitting into
the front and back of the next stitch, K2,
repeat from * to the last 2 stitches, K2.
Row 11: Purl.

There is now a change in the way you increase. Instead of knitting into the front and back of a stitch, you will now Make 1 (M1) — see page 15.

Row 12: K2, *K3, M1, K1, M1, K3, repeat from * to the last 2 stitches, K2.
Row 13: Purl.
Row 14: Knit.
Row 15: P2, *K4, P3, K4, repeat from * to last 2 stitches, P2.
Row 16: K2, *P4, M1, K1, M1, P4, repeat from * to last 2 stitches, K2.
Row 17: P2, *K4, P5, K4, repeat from * to last 2 stitches, P2.
Row 18: K2, *P4, K5, P4, repeat from * to last 2 stitches, P2.
Row 19: P2, *K4, P5, K4, repeat from * to last 2 stitches, P2.
Row 20: K2, *P4, K1, M1, K1, M1, K1, P4, repeat from * to last 2 stitches, K2.
Row 21: P2, *K4, P7, K4, repeat from * to last 2 stitches, P2.
Row 22: K2, *P4, K7, P4, repeat from * to last 2 stitches, K2.

USING THE GRAPH

Have a good look at your knitting in front of you with the right side facing. The rectangle blocks are made from the reverse side of stocking stitch. It is these blocks of reverse stocking stitch that you will weave the pink threads into with the crochet hook.

Have a good look at the graph on page 152. See how it matches your knitting up to Row 22.

Remember that you must always work 2 stitches at the beginning of the row, then knit the repeating pattern of the graph, and work 2 stitches at the end of the row. This will give you seams to work with when putting it all together.

Rows 23–52: Off you go and conquer the graph.

CASTING OFF

Use Jeny's Surprising Elastic Bind-Off (see page 14).

Weaving

Cut one ball of the Cerise wool and the Soft Powdery Pink kid mohair into approximately 12-cm (5-in) lengths. No need to be too particular about it. I wrapped the yarn around my open hand a few times and then cut and cut again. OK, so I have a wide spread. Use the 3 mm (UK 11, USA C) crochet hook to

thread the lengths, alternating the colours, through the bumpy stitches of the reverse stocking stitch blocks. Have a look at the picture. This activity will either spirit you away into a peaceful meditative state from which you will never want to return or it will send you nuts. Calm or crazy, La La Land isn't such a bad place I reckon.

Blocking

Block!

That means wet the knitted Sides and spread on a towel on the verandah. Pat each one out into a beautiful symmetrical flat thing. Leave to dry.

Gusset

The Gusset is the knitted strip that keeps the Sides apart and forms the base of the Le Grand Sac (or the top of Le Grand Couvre-théière). You should only knit it when you have blocked the Sides (have you?), because the measurements need to be precise.

Using 5 mm (UK 6, USA 8) needles and Cerise wool, cast on 10 stitches.
Row 1: K2, slip 2 purlwise (keeping the yarn at the back), K2, slip 2 purlwise (yarn at back), K2.
Row 2: P2, K2, P2, K2, P2.
Repeat these 2 rows until work measures the length of the outer arc of the blocked knitted Sides. Measure that outer arc once and twice and even thrice to be sure.

Paper template for the lining

BEFORE you sew the knitted Sides to the Gusset, make a paper template for the cotton fabric lining, using the diagram (opposite) as a guide.

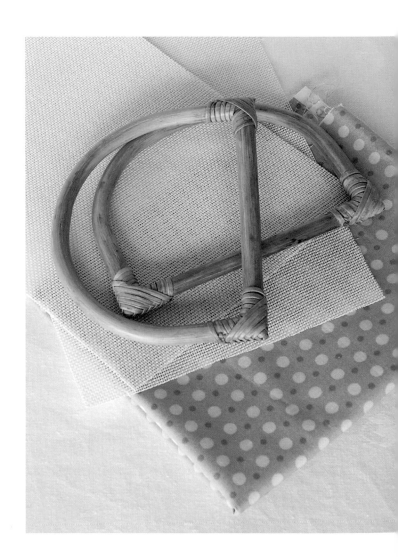

Measure the RADIUS, from the centre of one Side across the middle of the knitting. This spot is likely to be the least stretched. Get yourself a pair of compasses or a tack with a pencil on a string and draw a half-circle template to match the knitted Side. Cut the paper template, which should be geometrically accurate. The knitted Side may not be exactly right but it can be eased into shape later.

Measure, draw and cut a template for the handbag Gusset as well.

The cotton fabric lining

Cut 2 stiff interfacing pieces to the size of the half-circle Side template.

Cut 1 stiff interfacing piece to the size of the handbag Gusset.

Iron the sticky side of the interfacing down onto the wrong side of the cotton fabric leaving enough space around the templates to cut out extra seam allowance (indicated with dotted line).

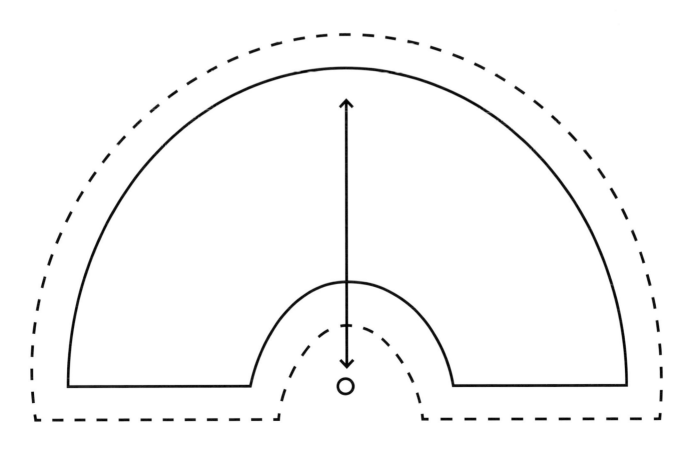

With right sides together, join one fabric Side to the fabric Gusset with pins. Sew the two pieces together with a cotton thread and a fine sewing needle. I used a simple overstitch. Keep it small and neat. You may be clever on a sewing machine, in which case go for it. I have some weird mental block in my sewing head, where the act of finding needle and thread and threading that needle seems simpler than messing with a great big lump of metal and electric cords. Somewhere in there, the equation of hand sewing time versus machine sewing time has completely escaped my logic.

Repeat for the other Side.

The knitted outer bag

With right sides together, join one knitted Side to the knitted Gusset with pins. Using a darning needle and the Cerise wool, sew the parts together using the simplest tacking stitch. Make a feature of the tacking stitch on the Manx Loaghtan by inserting the yarn down through the top of the cast-off edge. Play with it. See what you think. I am no sewing expert but I did try a few different stitches and found the simple tacking stitch to be the most effective, after all. Repeat the same for the other Side.

Knitted rim

Using 4 mm (UK 8, USA 6) needles and
Cerise wool, with the right side facing you,
pick up about 70 stitches around one edge of
the bag opening, from handle collar to handle
collar. The count is best divided into about
31 stitches along the front, 8 stitches across
where the Gusset meets the opening of the
bag and a further 31 stitches along the back.
Now, with the wrong side facing, knit the
next row. Purl a row. Knit a row. Continue
working in stocking stitch for 8 rows. The
wrong (purl) side of the stocking stitch is the
right side of the fabric. Cast off with Jeny's
Surprisingly Elastic Bind-Off (see page 14).

Repeat for the other end of the bag opening.

Putting it all together

Insert the lining into the knitted bag. Pin
the rolled (reverse stocking stitch) rim to the
very top of the lining edge closing up the roll
as you go. Using the cotton thread and the
sewing needle, stitch the rolled rim to the top
of the lining with small and secret stitches.
Repeat for the other side of the handle.

Wrap the centre rolled collars around
the cane handles and stitch into place
using the Manx Loaghtan yarn.

Make a simple twisted or plaited woollen
loop and use a button or a felted ball for
the catch. I bought this felted ball. In fact,
I bought a whole packet of felted balls to
play with. But one will do for The Bag.

Devilish

{KNITTED TEA COSY}

This bloody tea cosy! Really! Am I allowed to use the great Australian adjective in a tea cosy book? Well I just bloody well did.

This tea cosy had the devil in him and I had a devil of a time getting him out of my head and onto the teapot. I had to learn how to do short rows and I had to learn how to do short rows well and I had to learn how to pattern short rows and then I had to pontificate over, pore over, worry about how to explain short rows to you so that you would think they were EASY. Then I lost all my notes and diagrams and had to start all over again. The things I do for you. Yes. The things. It is not an easy life being a funny knitter, not at all.

BUT! Here he is. I've knitted an extra pair of horns for Wearing on Wednesdays and Washdays and While Wacuuming.

Size

To fit a six-cup teapot that stands 13 cm (5 in) tall (not including the knob) and 12 cm (4¾ in) in diameter (not including the spout and handle).

Materials

* 1 x 50 g (1¾ oz) ball Debbie Bliss Donegal Luxury Tweed Aran: Red
* 1 x 50 g (1¾ oz) ball Naturally Aran Tweed 10-ply: Olive
* 3 metres (3⅓ yards) chunky yarn or a heavily slubbed yarn for the rim around the horns

Note. It is not essential that you use these brands of yarn, but the deep earthy colours and the mottled colour speckling of the Aran tweed make it a bit special.

Equipment

* Two sets 6 mm (UK 4, USA 10) circular needles, 60 cm (24 in) long from needle tip to needle tip, for the Rim
* Two sets 5 mm (UK 6, USA 8) circular needles, 60 cm (24 in) long from needle tip to needle tip, for the Body
* One set 4 mm (UK 8, USA 6) circular needles, 80 cm (31½ in) long from needle tip to needle tip, for the Horns
* Polyester fibrefill
* Scissors
* Darning needle

Note. If you don't already have all these needle sizes in sets of two, and you want to save a bit of money, two sets of 5.5 mm (UK 5, USA 9) circular needles, 80 cm (31½ in) from needle tip to needle tip, will work for both the body of the cosy and for the chunky yarn rim around the horns. But I have a plethora of needles and this is what I used.

Method

The Horns are knitted on ONE SET of circular needles, using the Magic Loop method (see page 11). They also feature Short Rows (see below). The chunky Rim and tea cosy Body are knitted on TWO SETS of circular needles (see page 12).

About short rows

Adding short rows while knitting in the round gives the horns their curved shape.

Short rows are often used in sock patterns or to shape necklines. It is a very useful technique to have in your bag of tricks.

Very Important Note. If you haven't knitted short rows before, don't be shy. It is not hard, really it isn't. But it IS important to read the following instructions. Don't worry if they don't make complete sense to you on the first reading. They will when you begin knitting and you will feel VERY clever.

When knitting in the round, naturally you just go round and round and round. When a short ROW is added into the mix, the 'Wrap and Turn' (W&T) trick will ensure a smooth transition from knitting in the ROUND to knitting in ROWS.

W&T KNITWISE

Bring the yarn forward, slip the next stitch knitwise, take the yarn to the back, return the stitch back to left needle, TURN. Now you are ready to purl the short row.

W&T PURLWISE

Take the yarn to the back, slip the next stitch purlwise, bring the yarn to the front, return the stitch to left needle. (Keep this purlwise wrap loose for an easy pick up later.) TURN and continue knitting in the round.

HIDING THE WRAP ON THE WAY BACK

The next fabulous technique belongs to Cat Bordhi.

You can just knit straight across the wrapped stitch when you come back to it OR you can hide it. To hide the wrap, pick it up and take it back over the stitch it is wrapping on the left needle. Both stitches should have their legs open rather than crossed. Weeelllll (said in low growly voice). You ARE making a devil. Then knit those two stitches together through the back of the loops like an SSK. My abbreviation for this action is PUwrap K2tog tbl.

Another abbreviation

M1 = Make 1 (see page 15).

Peaked horn (make 2)

Using 4 mm (UK 8, USA 6) needles and Donegal Tweed Aran, cast on 6 stitches.

Note. Mark the beginning of the round with a contrasting coloured tie. It helps keep confusion at bay. I certainly need all the help I can get.

Rounds 1 & 2: Knit.
Round 3: (K1, M1, K2) twice.
Round 4: (K3, M1, K1) twice.
Round 5: (K1, M1, K4) twice (12 sts).
Rounds 6–8: Knit.

Round 9: K1, W&T knitwise, P8, W&T purlwise, knit to end of round.
Round 10: K1, PUwrap K2tog tbl, K2, PUwrap K2tog tbl, knit to end of round.
Round 11: Knit.
Round 12: *K1, M1, K1, repeat from * to end of round.
Rounds 13–15: Knit.

Round 16: K2, W&T knitwise, P13, W&T purlwise, knit to end of round.
Round 17: K2, PUwrap K2tog tbl, K3, PUwrap K2tog tbl, knit to end of round.
Round 18: Knit.
Round 19: *K1, M1, K2, repeat from * to end of round.
Rounds 20–22: Knit.

Round 23: K3, W&T knitwise, P18, W&T purlwise, knit to end of round.
Round 24: K3 PUwrap K2tog tbl, K4, PUwrap K2tog tbl, knit to end of round.
Round 25: Knit.
Round 26: *K1, M1, K3, repeat from * to end of round.
Rounds 27–29: Knit.

Round 30: K4, W&T knitwise, P23, W&T purlwise, knit to end of round.
Round 31: K4, PUwrap K2tog tbl, K5, PUwrap K2tog tbl, knit to end of round.
Round 32: Knit.
Round 33: *K1, M1, K4, repeat from * to end of round.
Rounds 34–36: Knit.

Round 37: K5, W&T knitwise, P28, W&T purlwise, knit to end of round.
Round 38: K5, PUwrap K2tog tbl, K6, PUwrap K2tog tbl, knit to end of round.
Round 39: Knit.
Round 40: *K1, M1, K5, repeat from * to end of round.
Rounds 41–43: Knit.

Round 44: K6, W&T knitwise, P33, W&T purlwise, knit to end of round.
Round 45: K6, PUwrap K2tog tbl, K7, PUwrap K2tog tbl, knit to end of round.
Round 46: Knit.
Round 47: *K1, M1, K6, repeat from * to end of round.
Rounds 48–50: Knit.

Round 51: *K1, M1, K7, repeat from * to end of round.
Rounds 52–54: Knit.

When you have finished one horn, cut the thread, leaving a long end — enough to knit 6 stitches and then some to darn in later. Move the stitches onto a couple of stitch holders or onto another set of circular needles while you knit up the second horn.

Leave the yarn intact on the second horn ready for grafting.

SET UP TO GRAFT TWO HORNS TOGETHER

Think of the horns as having a front and a back for this purpose. If you are at the beginning of a round you will be ready to knit the front. The front is the concave curve, the bit curling under. Knit 6 stitches. If you are using the Two Sets of Circular Needles method (see page 12), knit those 6 stitches with

the needles that are holding the back stitches. Count 15 stitches on the front set of needles and slip the remaining 6 stitches to the back set of needles. You should now have 39 stitches on the back set of circular needles and 15 stitches on the front set of circular needles.

JOINING THE TWO HORNS TO EACH OTHER WITH A GRAFT AND CAST OFF

Line up the fronts, the concave curves, so they are facing each other. Graft with the wrong side of the knitted fabric facing you. You should be peering into the holes of the horns while you graft and cast off. Line up both sets of needles with the tips together at the end where your working thread is.

Knit 2 stitches together, one from the front set of needles and one from the back set of needles.

Knit the second two together, one from the front set of needles and one from the back set of needles.

Lift the back stitch over the front stitch on the working needles to cast off.

Knit the next two stitches together, one from the front set of needles and one from the back set of needles.

Lift the back stitch over the front stitch on the working needles to cast off.

Continue until you have one stitch left. Cut the yarn and pull the thread through the last stitch.

With the right side facing and using 6 mm (UK 4, USA 10) circular needles and chunky wool, knit one round. Purl two rounds. Cast off purlwise.

Body (make 1)

Worked in ROUNDS from the top down. There is no need to make a lining for this Body. The New Zealand Naturally Aran Tweed 10-ply will be sturdy enough as will the wide spread of the horn structure.

Using both sets of 6 mm (UK 4, USA 10) circular needles and Naturally Aran Tweed 10-ply, cast on 8 stitches and join in the round. Proceed as for the **Basic Tea Cosy** (see page 16). I used the K2, P2 rib pattern.

Putting it all together

Put it all together! No, no. Just kidding. But you don't need instructions about darning in ends and sewing up any recalcitrant holes and stuffing horns with fibrefill and placing them just so on the cosy body while the cosy body is sitting on the pot and then sewing them on. Do you?

Lily of the Valley

{KNITTED TEA COSY WITH OPTIONAL CROCHET FLORET}

For You

Lily requires a lot of wool and the Noro Kureyon is not inexpensive BUT, isn't she glorious. She will last many lifetimes, proprietarily whisked away when you leave for the great tea party in the sky, linking generation after generation with a woolly thread to your heart. And if Lily must be a gift, then she is the perfect gift for the girl who has everything, or the girl who deserves everything.

Size

To fit a six-cup teapot that stands 13 cm (5 in) tall (not including the knob) and 12 cm (4¾ in) in diameter (not including the spout and handle).

Materials

* 4 x 50 g (1¾ oz) balls Noro Kureyon wool, for Petals (see Note below)
* 2 x 50 g (1¾ oz) balls Noro Kureyon wool, for Florets
* 1 x 50 g (1¾ oz) ball Nundle Collection 8-ply wool, for the lining

Note. I haven't given you colour descriptions because Noro colours constantly change. Choose the hues you love best and play with those.

Equipment

* One set 4 mm (UK 8, USA 6) circular needles, 80 cm (31½ in) long from needle tip to needle tip
* One set 5 mm (UK 6, USA 8) circular needles, 80 cm (31½ in) long from needle tip to needle tip
* 5 mm (UK 6, USA 8H) crochet hook
* Darning needle
* Scissors
* Flower head pins

Method

Knitted in the ROUND.
I used the Magic Loop method (see page 11) for the Petals and the Body.

Body (make 1)

Worked in ROUNDS from the top down.
Using one set of 4 mm (UK 8, USA 6) circular needles and Nundle Collection 8-ply, cast on 8 stitches. Join in the round (see page 13). Proceed as for the **Basic Tea Cosy** on page 16.

Large petals (make 10)

Note. You might notice that not all my petals are exactly the same size. If you want to vary the size of your petals then be game. Simply add or take away the number of plain knitting rounds in between the increasing and decreasing rounds. After two or three times of knitting the petal to my template you'll get the idea.

Using 5 mm (UK 6, USA 8) circular needles and Noro Kureyon wool, cast on 12 stitches and join in the round.

For the increasing pattern, work as follows:
Rounds 1 & 2: (K5, P1) twice.
Round 3: (K2, M1 (see page 15), K1, M1, K2, P1) twice.
Rounds 4 & 5: (K7, P1) twice.
Round 6: (K3, M1, K1, M1, K3, P1) twice.
Rounds 7 & 8: (K9, P1) twice.
Round 9: (K4, M1, K1, M1, K4, P1) twice.

Rounds 10 & 11: (K11, P1) twice.
Round 12: (K5, M1, K1, M1, K5, P1) twice.
Rounds 13 & 14: (K13, P1) twice.
Round 15: (K6, M1, K1, M1, K6, P1), twice.
Rounds 16 & 17: (K15, P1) twice.
Round 18: (K7, M1, K1, M1, K7, P1) twice (36 sts).
Rounds 19–22: (K17, P1) twice.

For the decreasing pattern, work as follows:
Round 23: (K6, ssk, K1, K2tog, K6, P1) twice.
Rounds 24–26: (K15, P1) twice.
Round 27: (K5, ssk, K1, K2tog, K5, P1) twice.
Rounds 28–30: (K13, P1) twice.
Round 31: (K4, ssk, K1, K2tog, K4, P1) twice.
Rounds 32–34: (K11, P1) twice.
Round 35: (K3, ssk, K1, K2tog, K3, P1) twice.
Rounds 36–38: (K9, P1) twice.
Round 39: (K2, ssk, K1, K2tog, K2, P1) twice.
Rounds 40–42: (K7, P1) twice.
Round 43: (K1, ssk, K1, K2tog, K1, P1) twice (12 sts).

Now it changes a little bit.
Rounds 44 & 45: (K5, P1) twice.
Round 46: (ssk, K1, K2tog, P1) twice.
Round 47: (K3, P1) twice.
Round 48: ssk, K2tog, ssk, K2tog (4 sts).
Cut a long piece of yarn and draw it up through the remaining 4 stitches to a nice point.

Smaller petals (make 6)

Using 5 mm (UK 6, USA 8) circular needles and Noro Kureyon wool, cast on 8 stitches and join in the round.

For the increasing pattern, work as follows:
Rounds 1 & 2: (K3, P1) twice.
Round 3: (K1, M1, K1, M1, K1, P1) twice.
Rounds 4 & 5: (K5, P1) twice.
Round 6: (K2, M1, K1, M1, K2, P1) twice.
Rounds 7 & 8: (K7, P1) twice.
Round 9: (K3, M1, K1, M1, K3, P1) twice.
Rounds 10 & 11: (K9, P1) twice.
Round 12: (K4, M1, K1, M1, K4, P1) twice (24 sts).
Rounds 13 & 14: (K11, P1) twice.

For the decreasing pattern, work as follows:
Round 15: (K3, ssk, K1, K2tog, K3, P1) twice.

Rounds 16–18: (K9, P1) twice.
Round 19: (K2, ssk, K1,
K2tog, K2, P1) twice.
Rounds 20–22: (K7, P1) twice.
Round 23: (K1, ssk, K1,
K2tog, K1, P1) twice.

Now it changes a little bit.
Rounds 24 & 25: (K5, P1) twice.
Round 26: (ssk, K1, K2tog, P1) twice.
Round 27: (K3, P1) twice.
Round 28: ssk, K2tog, ssk, K2tog (4 sts).
Cut a long yarn end and draw it up through
the remaining 4 stitches to a nice point.

FINISHING THE PETALS

Thread the yarn onto a darning needle
and secure the two sides of the petal
together down the centre with a simple
tacking stitch. The centre or vein of the
leaf is where the increasing and decreasing
took place. Make sure you line up the
centres exactly. The purl stitch gives an
easy crease at the edges of the leaf.

Floret {crocheted}

*Note. American crocheters, Australian/English
crochet language is different to American crochet
language. An Australian/English dc, or double
crochet, is the same as an American sc, or single
crochet. True! You had better check the Crochet
Abbreviations and terms table on page 156.*

Using a 5 mm (UK 6, USA 8H) crochet
hook and Noro Kureyon wool, make
4 chain. Sl st into first chain to close the
circle. Make 1 ch (counts as first dc). Make
6 dc into the circle. At the end of the first
round, simply make the next dc into the
first sl stitch and continue to work in a spiral
(not in brick walls as you might if you were
working back and forth across rows).

To make the cone shapes, you will
gradually increase. Increase by making
2 dc into 1 dc in the round below. I'll leave
the number of increases up to you. This
is sculptural crochet and, like clay, if it
doesn't turn out the way you want you can
just throw the clay again and reshape it.

To finish off each of the cones, sl st the last
two stitches, break off the yarn and draw it
through that last loop and pull tightly. With

the crochet hook, loop the remaining thread through the next two or three stitches of the bottom edge and snip short the yarn end.

When you have 5 or 6 fat little cone shapes, sew them together at the base. The first three or four might be a bit fiddly but it gets easier as it grows. Then keep crocheting those cones. You may need as many as 30 or even 40. Keep trying it on your pot. Best to do all this part last when you have made the Body and the Petals and put all that together the way you want. This will determine the number and placing of the cones in the floret.

Putting it all together

Darn in all the ends. Place the Body on the teapot to measure and sew the seams together under the handle and spout.

Pin the inside Large Petals to the Body. Pin the outside Large Petals to the Body. Pin the Smaller Petals under the handle and spout first and then the remaining couple around the lower edges. Don't be too symmetrical at this point.

Notice I have not said to sew anything except the Body seams. It is very important to pin and play, play and pin. Make sure that you are happy with the way it is all sitting. Adjust. When you ARE satisfied, take away all the petals but two. Sew them into place. Then pin the remaining Large Petals into place again. When you are happy, remove all but two more petals and sew them into place. Take your time. Sleep on it.

This is the key to making all your efforts shine.

Egg Daisies

{KNITTED EGG COSY}

OK OK, so I have gone all cute on you. I can do cute.
Briefly, in a small inoffensive egg cosy sort of way.

Size

To fit extra large organic free-range chicken eggs.

Materials

* 1 x 50 g (1¾ oz) ball Shelter wool: Thistle (see Note below)
* A little bit of yellow for the centre pompom

Note. One 50 g (1¾ oz) ball of wool will make two cosies. For the yellow, I used a 4-ply (fingering weight) hand-dyed yarn bought on holidays in Tasmania three years ago. That yellow has been waiting for its moment in the sun all that time. Oh, and I also used a bit of Moda Vera merino mohair blend: Mustard.

Equipment

* One set 4 mm (UK 8, USA 6) circular needles, 80 cm (31½ in) long from needle tip to needle tip
* Darning needle
* Scissors
* Pompom maker, 3.5 cm (1½ in) diameter. Every modern knitter should have a pompom maker

Method

Knitted in the ROUND.
I used the Magic Loop method
for this job (see page 11).

Petals (make 5)

Using 4 mm (UK 8, USA 6) circular
needles and Shelter wool, cast on
8 stitches and join in the round.

For the increasing pattern, work as follows:
Rounds 1 & 2: (K3, P1) twice.
Round 3: (K1, M1 (see page 15),
K1, M1, K1, P1) twice.
Rounds 4 & 5: (K5, P1) twice.
Round 6: (K2, M1, K1,
M1, K2, P1) twice.
Rounds 7 & 8: (K7, P1) twice.
Round 9: (K3, M1, K1,
M1, K3, P1) twice.
Rounds 10 & 11: (K9, P1) twice.
Round 12: (K4, M1, K1,
M1, K4, P1) twice.
Rounds 13 & 14: (K11, P1) twice.
Round 15: (K5, M1, K1, M1,
K5, P1) twice (28 sts).
Rounds 16 & 17: (K13, P1) twice.

For the decreasing pattern, work as follows:
Round 18: (K4, ssk, K1,
K2tog, K4, P1) twice.
Rounds 19–21: (K11, P1) twice.
Round 22: (K3, ssk, K1,
K2tog, K3, P1) twice.
Rounds 23–25: (K9, P1) twice.
Round 26: (K2, ssk, K1,
K2tog, K2, P1) twice.
Rounds 27–29: (K7, P1) twice.
Round 30: (K1, ssk, K1,
K2tog, K1, P1) twice.

Now it changes a little bit.
Rounds 31 & 32: (K5, P1) twice.
Round 33: (ssk, K1, K2tog, P1) twice.
Round 34: (K3, P1) twice.
Round 35: ssk, K2tog, ssk, K2tog (4 sts).
Cut a long yarn end and draw it up through
the remaining 4 stitches to a nice point.

Putting it all together

Stretch and spread the petals into shape. The column of increases and decreases forms the centre vein of the petal. The two columns of purl stitches form the outside edges of the petal. Line up the petal veins front and back. Thread the long yarn end onto a darning needle and secure the front vein to the back vein with a simple tacking stitch, checking all the while that the veins are lined up exactly.

Iron. Sacrilege I know, ironing wool. But what the heck! It works. Use a steam iron on wool temperature and iron from the base of the petal (the fatter end) up towards the pointy bit. Hold the very tip of the petal while you iron upwards to help stretch it out long. Don't burn yourself!

Make the pompom. In One's vast experience of making pompoms, One has discovered that even the fanciest of pompom-making gadgets does not produce a perfectly spherical pompom. One needs to use One's sharpest scissors, and One's eye, to trim it up.

The short fat ends of the petals meet at the centre of the daisy. Layer one short fat end over another short fat end. You want to form a bowl rather than a flat mat. Pin all the petals together first and measure for size over an egg in an eggcup. It will help give you an idea of how much overlap is needed.

Take the pins out. They'll just get in the way now. Anyhow, you want to add one petal at a time. Start at the top of the first two short fat ends with an overstitch. Make a secret tacking stitch down the short fat ends, to not quite half way, by sewing the bottom part of the top petal to the top part of the bottom petal. Join the other three petals in the same way.

If none of that makes any sense … look at the picture and trust your costume making skills. It is all just smoke and mirrors really.

Tie the pompom to the centre.

Everyone will want one, so off you go now and make 500 more petals.

Tammy Shanter

{KNITTED TEA COSY}

For Harry

Harry was my maternal grandfather. He is my Scottish heritage. My red hair. My flammable nature. Who can you blame if you can't blame dead kin? So here it is. Knitted argyle. For Harry, affectionately known as Dinsy. I liked him a lot.

Size

To fit a six-cup teapot that stands 14 cm (5½ in) tall (not including the knob) and 14 cm (5½ in) in diameter (not including the spout and handle).

Materials

* 2 x 50 g (1¾ oz) balls Shelter wool, Main Colour (MC): Long Johns
* 2 x 50 g (1¾ oz) balls Shelter wool, Contrast Colour (CC): Fossil
* 1 x 50 g (1¾ oz) ball Nundle 8-ply wool, for Lining

Equipment

* Two sets 4 mm (UK 8, USA 6) circular needles, 60 cm (24 in) long from needle tip to needle tip
* Darning needle
* Scissors
* Pompom maker, 5 cm (2 in) diameter
* Small amount polyester fibrefill
* Stiff interfacing

Method

Knitted in the ROUND. I used the TWO SETS of circular needles for this job (see page 12). That sounds innocent enough. It also involves an Argyle pattern and steeking (see below). Mmmmm …

Argyle

Argyle has been done many times in many ways, but before venturing to call anything my own, I searched high and low for the 'original' Argyle print. Argyle seems to be repeated, reiterated, rehashed, reinvented, rewound, reunited and reverberated. So without trepidation, I offer you this Argyle print, most probably seen before but not yet found on a tea cosy. Well, I haven't found it on a tea cosy anyway.

Steeking warning

What is steeking I hear you ask? It is cutting the knitted fabric. It is something you do after knitting Fair Isle in the round. I haven't lost you yet have I? Take a deep breath. You are not alone. I have seen experienced, proficient knitters have palpitations at the THOUGHT of cutting the knitted fabric they have just spent hours creating.

   No palpitations? Good. Off you go then. The rest of you? When you get to the steeking bit — have a cup of tea. Remember. It is small. It is forgiving. You don't have to wear it. No one you know has to wear it. It is a TEA COSY for goodness sake. The perfect little bit of nonsense to try something

new on and, if at the end you don't feel extremely pleased with yourself, and don't want to just run off and steek yourself a whole wardrobe of cardigans, then I'll … I'll … well, I'll eat my Tammy Shanter.

Cosy

BODY
Using both sets of 4 mm (UK 8, USA 6) circular needles and MC (Long Johns), cast on 92 stitches. Join in the round.

Important Note. In your knitty head, and so that you know what you are doing, compartmentalise the stitches thus:

The first set of circular needles: The first 6 stitches are the steeking and hemming segment, the next 40 stitches follow the Argyle pattern. Repeat the Argyle pattern as needed.

The second set of circular needles: The first 6 stitches are the steeking and hemming segment and again, the next 40 stitches follow the Argyle pattern from the BEGINNING of the chart (see opposite). The Argyle pattern does NOT fit neatly into the TOTAL 80 stitches in the round. Starting at the beginning of the Argyle chart on each set of circular needles solves that little hiccup of maths.

Rounds 1–10: K6, *P2, K2, repeat from * to end of first set of circular needles, K6, *P2, K2, repeat from * to end of second set of circular needles.
Round 11: Knit.

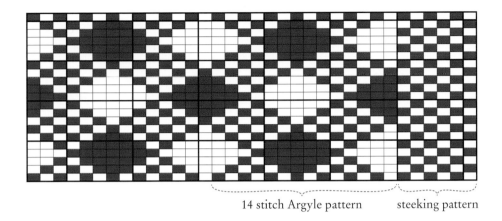

14 stitch Argyle pattern   steeking pattern

ARGYLE PATTERN

Rounds 12–32: Join in CC (Fossil) and follow the chequerboard pattern on the graph above for the Steeking stitches, followed by the Argyle pattern, for these 21 rounds.

LOSING THE STEEKING AND HEMMING STITCHES FROM THE NEEDLES

I have started the count at 1 again because, frankly, I can.

ROUND 1 (SPOKEN WITH A SCOOTISH ACCENT):

Break off CC, leaving a long thread to darn in later. *Knit the first 6 stitches, then slip those 6 stitches onto a small stitch holder or a piece of bright pink wool, like I have.

Using MC, knit to the end of the first set of circular needles. Repeat from * for the second set of circular needles.

JOINING UP AGAIN OVER THE STEEKING SECTION

You will continue working in the round straight across the gap left by the steeking section. To make a firm join at this point, slip the working needle tip into the first stitch of the round and then into the back of the last stitch of the previous round (sitting on the now sleeping set of needles) and knit as if to knit 2 together.

Rounds 2–11: *K2, P2, repeat from * to end of round.

UNDERSIDE OF THE TAMMY

Join in CC. Leave MC attached, but don't take it with you on your journey round the next 4 rounds. Just weave it in at the back for one stitch each time you reach the beginning of the round again so that it is ready and waiting for you when you need it.
Round 12: Knit.
Round 13: *K7, M1 (see page 15), repeat from * to end of round.

Round 14: Knit.
Round 15: *K8, M1, repeat from * to end of round.

SETTING UP THE HEART MOTIF

Round 16: *K5 (CC), K1 (MC), K3 (CC), repeat from * to end of round.

Yes, the Contrast Colour looks like it ought to be called the Main Colour and the Main Colour looks like it ought to be called the Contrast Colour. Forget all that. Look at the graph below or the picture on page 63 and follow your instinct and all will be well. You now have the bottom points of the little hearts set up. The rest is easy. Really it is. Follow the colour Heart motif chart below AT THE SAME TIME as the increasing pattern thus:

Round 17: *K9, M1, repeat from * to end of round.
Round 18 (and each

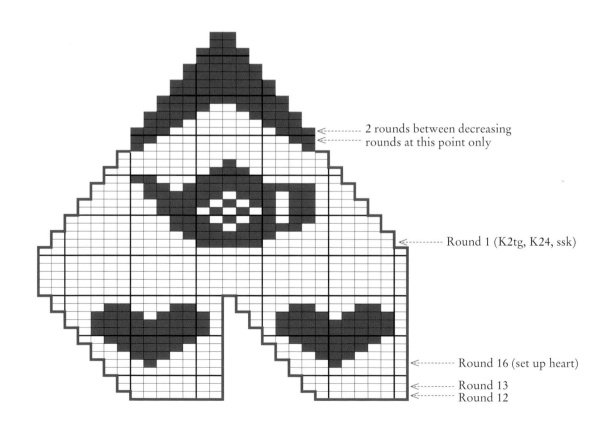

←------- 2 rounds between decreasing
←------- rounds at this point only

←------- Round 1 (K2tg, K24, ssk)

←------- Round 16 (set up heart)
←------- Round 13
←------- Round 12

alternate round): Knit.
Round 19: *K10, M1, repeat from * to end of round.
Round 21: *K11, M1, repeat from * to end of round.
Round 23: *K12, M1, repeat from * to end of round.
Round 25: *K13, M1, repeat from * to end of round.
Rounds 26–30: Knit.
You will have 84 stitches on each cable, 168 stitches in total.

DECREASING FOR THE CROWN

(The count begins again at 1.
Mwahhh haw haw)
Continue using CC.

SETTING UP THE TEAPOT MOTIF

Round 1: *K2tog (CC), K9 (CC), K5 (MC), K10 (CC), ssk (MC), repeat from * to end of round.

Again, follow the colour Teapot and Star motif chart (opposite) AT THE SAME TIME as the decreasing pattern thus:
Round 2 (and each alternate round): Knit.
Round 3: *K2tog, K22, ssk, repeat from * to end of round.
Round 5: *K2tog, K20, ssk, repeat from * to end of round.
Round 7: *K2tog, K18, ssk, repeat from * to end of round.
Round 9: *K2tog, K16, ssk,

repeat from * to end of round.
Round 11: *K2tog, K14, ssk, repeat from * to end of round.

SETTING UP THE STAR MOTIF

Follow the colour Teapot and Star motif chart AT THE SAME TIME as the decreasing pattern thus:
Round 13: *K2tog (MC), K12 (CC), ssk (MC), repeat from * to end of round.
Round 14: *K2 (MC), K10 (CC), K2 (MC), repeat from * to end of round.
Round 15: *K3 (MC), K8 (CC), K3 (MC), repeat from * to end of round.

(YES, there are two non-decreasing rounds onc after the other. Rounds 14 and 15. Just this once though. It helps set up the star chart nicely.)

Round 16: *K2tog, K10, ssk, repeat from * to end of round.
Round 17 (and each alternate round): Knit.
Round 18: *K2tog, K8, ssk, repeat from * to end of round.
Continue in this decreasing pattern while following the colour graph until there are 12 stitches remaining.
Last round: *K2tog, repeat from * to end of round.
Break off yarn, leaving a long end to thread through the remaining stitches and darn in.

Steeking and hemming

Find the centre of the 6 steeking stitches and mark with a contrasting thread with a simple large tacking stitch. You will have 3 columns of stitches on one side of the marker and 3 columns of stitches on the other. Don't be confused by the last 2 knit stitches of the ribbing in the Argyle section.

Working from the bottom up, sew the first column of stitches out from the centre to the second column of stitches out from the centre, using blanket stitch (see page 15). Don't miss any knit stitches. The point of the exercise is to prevent the knitted stitches from unravelling. I have used a 4-ply yarn, still in a contrasting colour. You could, of course, get out your sewing machine and zigzag your way up. Up to you. I did it by hand.

When you get to the top, secure the 3 loose stitches on this side of the steeking centre with the blanket stitch also.
    Repeat it all for the other side of the centre marker.
    Get those scissors out. Sharp scissors. Remove the centre marker and cut along the same line. Fold those hems back under and pin into place.

Join the bottom ribbing together (below the spout and handle openings) using mattress stitch (see page 14). Then use a simple loose tacking stitch to secure the fold back into place. You may need a stitch or two at the top of the spout and handle opening too.

Feel very clever. Feel very, very clever.

Lining

Yes yes yes. Make the lining. After all that cleverness, you want it to sit well and look fabulous.

Using 4 mm (UK 8, USA 6) circular needles and 8-ply yarn, cast on 8 stitches.

Proceed as for the **Basic Tea Cosy** on page 16.

Putting it all together

Make a pompom and attach it to the top of the crown.

Spread the fibrefill lightly across the inside of the crown. Cut the stiff interfacing to size and insert it in the crown.

Wherever a Scootsmn (that's a Scotsman to you) is in the world, he'll feel right at home with one of these on the teapot.

Eugenie

{KNITTED TEA COSY}

For Princess Eugenie and a Royal wedding

*What else can I say except that it is Eugenie's
turn to steal the limelight.*

Size

To fit a six-cup teapot that stands 11 cm (4½ in)
tall (not including the knob) and 14 cm (5½ in)
in diameter (not including the spout and handle).
The best sort of pot for the Pillbox Princesses
is a round-bellied, flat-top teapot, the sort that
the Chinese produce a million million of.

Materials

* 4 x 50 g (1¾ oz) balls Debbie Bliss
  Donegal Luxury Tweed Aran: Ice Blue
* 1 x 50 g (1¾ oz) ball Filatura
  di Crosa Zara: White
* 1 white feather
* 50 x 50 cm (20 x 20 in) very stiff,
  non-iron-on interfacing, for lining

Equipment

* Two sets 4 mm (UK 8, USA 6)
  circular needles, 60 cm (24 in)
  long from needle tip to needle tip
* Darning needle
* Fine sewing needle and cotton
* Scissors
* Tape measure
* Flower head pins
* Pencil
* Large safety pin

Method

Pillboxes knitted in the ROUND. I used TWO SETS of circular needles (see page 12). Twirly Fascinator knitted on the straight with ONE SET of circular needles.

Body

Using 4 mm (UK 8, USA 6) circular needles and Ice Blue yarn, cast on 8 stitches and join in the round.

Proceed as for the **Basic Tea Cosy** on page 16, for 10 rounds.

WHITE RIM

Join in the White yarn, and knit one round. Work the Wood Fungus variation (see page 18), as follows:
Purl one Round.

Return to the Ice Blue yarn and complete the **Basic Tea Cosy** pattern. I used the K2, P2 rib pattern.

Lining

The Lining is a must. Be sure to do both a Body and a Lining before you do anything else. The architecture on top will need that engineering on the bottom. Using 4 mm (UK 8, USA 6) circular needles and Ice Blue yarn, cast on 8 stitches and join in the round.

Proceed as for the **Basic Tea Cosy** on page 16.

Pillbox hat (make 3: large, medium and small)

The three pillbox constructions come in Large, Medium and Small sizes. Begin with the largest one, which will sit directly on the cosy on the pot.

CROWN (ALL SIZES)

Worked in ROUNDS from the top down.

Using 4 mm (UK 8, USA 6) circular needles and Ice Blue yarn, cast on 8 stitches. Join in the round.

Round 1 (and each alternate round): Knit.
Round 2: Increase by knitting into the front and back of each stitch.
Round 4: *K1, increase in next stitch, repeat from * to end of round.
Round 6: *K2, increase in next stitch, repeat from * to end of round.
Round 8: *K3, increase in next stitch, repeat from * to end of round.
Round 10: *K4, increase in next stitch, repeat from * to end of round.

Large size: Continue in this increasing pattern until there are 8 stitches in each segment of the pie — 32 stitches on each set of circular needles, a total of 64 stitches.
Medium size: Continue in this increasing pattern until there are 7 stitches in each segment — 28 stitches on each set of circular needles, a total of 54 stitches.

Small size: Continue in this increasing pattern until there are 6 stitches in each segment — 24 stitches on each set of circular needles, a total of 48 stitches.

TOP RIM (ALL SIZES)

Join in White yarn.
Knit one round.
Purl one round.

OUTER SIDE (ALL SIZES)

Return to Ice Blue yarn.
Knit one round.

Change to flat ribbing, as follows:
Round 1: *K2, P2, repeat from * to end of round.
Round 2: *K2, slip 2 purlwise (keeping the yarn at the back of the work), repeat from * to end of round.

Large and Medium sizes: Repeat the last 2 rounds a further 4 times (10 rounds of flat ribbing in all).
Small size: Repeat the last 2 rounds a further 3 times (8 rounds of flat ribbing in all).

BOTTOM RIM (ALL SIZES)

Join in White yarn.
Knit one round.
Purl one round.

Return to the Ice Blue yarn.
Knit one round.

INNER SIDE

Large and Medium sizes: Knit 8 rounds.
Small size: Knit 6 rounds.
All sizes: Cast off, using Jeny's Surprisingly Elastic Bind-Off (see page 14).

Pillbox lining

MEASURING AND CUTTING

An easy way to measure the circle size is to place your tape measure on the table and then place the knitted pillbox hat, upside down, on top. Stretch the Crown out with a splay of your fingers. Depending on the wool you have used and the tension of your knitting, you should have a diameter of about 15–16 cm (6–6½ in). Halve that figure and you have the radius of your circle. Use a pair of compasses, or a pencil on a string, to draw out a perfect circle shape on the stiff interfacing. It is preferable to cut it a little bit bigger than you need, as you can always cut a bit off, but you can't stick a bit back on. When you have cut the Crown interfacing, test it inside the knitted Crown and cut it down further if needed.

Mark your cutting lines with a pencil first.

Once you are satisfied that the Crown measurement is correct, wrap the tape measure around the circumference (approximately 52 cm or 20½ in) to measure the circumference of the sides. Add 2 cm (1 in) extra for a lap-over join.

Measure the width of the sides on the pillbox, from the Top Rim to the Bottom Rim (approximately 4 cm or 1½ in). Again, make it a little bit bigger. Test the side interfacing inside the knitted rim and cut it down to size if need be. A little stretch in the knitted fabric is a good thing.

PUTTING THE LINING IN THE PILLBOX

Try the side interfacing again for good measure. Then join it into a circle with a few well-placed stitches, using the fine sewing needle and cotton. Pop it into the rim of the hat and fold the stocking stitch up and over it. Using the same yarn and a darning needle, sew the inside knitted fabric to the outside knitted fabric where the crown meets the rim, WITHOUT catching the interfacing as you go. Place the circle lining up inside the Crown. It should tuck nicely above the rim interfacing.

Twirly fascinator

Using one set of 4 mm (UK 8, USA 6) needles and White yarn, cast on 110 stitches.
Join in the Ice Blue yarn and knit one row.
Change to flat ribbing (in Ice Blue) as follows:
Row 1: *K2, P2, repeat from * to end of row.
Row 2: *P2, slip 2 purlwise,

repeat from * to end of row.
Repeat these last 2 rows a further
4 times (10 rows of ribbing in all).

Row 11: Join in the White yarn
and knit to end of row.
Row 12: Purl.
Row 13: Knit.

Change to flat ribbing (in White) as follows:
Row 14: *K2, P2, repeat
from * to end of row.
Row 15: *P2, slip 2 purlwise,
repeat from * to end of row.
Repeat these last 2 rows a further
4 times (10 rows of ribbing in all).

Cast off normally, but loosely.
Using the White yarn, sew the cast-on edge
to the cast-off edge to form a long tube.
A simple tacking stitch from front to back
should do it.

Lightly iron the tube to make it flat and
to accentuate the white purl edging.

SHAPING THE STIFF INTERFACING

The stiff interfacing is NOT cut in a straight
line. No, no, no! To measure and shape the
interfacing, place the knitted tube directly
onto the interfacing in the shape of a circle.
Mark the outer edge of the circle you have
made with a pencil. This will become the
inner edge of the interfacing circle. Measure
the width of the knitted tube (approximately
4 cm or 1½ in). Measure and mark a wider
circumference, 4 cm (1½ in) out from
the circle you have already and cut.

Put the large safety pin in one end of
the interfacing twirly length and thread
through the knitted tube. Mould the knitted
tube into place so that the purl rims all
sit snug at the edges of the interfacing.

Putting it all together

The rest is up to you. Play! It is all smoke
and mirrors and feathers and twirling.
Whatever takes your fancy. I have only
one piece of advice. Well, two. BE
GAME! And pin before you sew.

Beatrice

{KNITTED TEA COSY}

For Princess Beatrice

Funny girls aren't they, those royal sisters.

Size

To fit a six-cup teapot that stands 11 cm (4½ in) tall (not including the knob) and 14 cm (5½ in) in diameter (not including the spout and handle).

Materials

* 2 x 25 g (⅞ oz) balls Sublime Kid Mohair Blend: Dusty Pink
* 2 x 50 g (1¾ oz) balls Filatura di Crosa Zarina: White
* 1 x 50 g (1¾ oz) ball Moda Vera Medley (a pink-and-beige loopy yarn used only for the twirly fascinator edging)
* 2 felted balls OR 2 small pompoms OR 2 fabulous buttons
* 2 mm (⅛ in) thick bonsai wire
* Plastic tubing with inner diameter just wide enough to fit the bonsai wire
* 50 x 50 cm (20 x 20 in) stiff, non-iron-on interfacing, for lining

Equipment

* Two sets 4 mm (UK 8, USA 6) circular needles, 60 cm (24 in) long from needle tip to needle tip
* Darning needle
* Sewing needle and cotton
* Scissors
* Tape measure
* Flower head pins

Method

Pillbox knitted in the ROUND. I used TWO SETS of circular needles (see page 12). Twirly Fascinator knitted on the straight with ONE SET of circular needles.

THE SAME AS EUGENIE

(Well they ARE sisters). Everything is pretty much the same as for Eugenie except, believe it or not, for Beatrice — less is more.

OK, so she is much the same except for the Twirly Fascinator.

Twirly fascinator (make 2: one in White (lining) and one in Dusty Pink (outer)).

Using one set of 4 mm (UK 8, USA 6) needles and Dusty Pink, cast on 110 stitches.
Row 1: Knit to end of row.
Change to flat ribbing as follows:
Row 2: *K2, P2, repeat from * to end of row.
Row 3: *P2, slip 2 purlwise, repeat from * to end of row.
Repeat these last 2 rows a further 4 times (10 rows of ribbing in all).

Row 11: Join in the Medley loopy yarn (leave the Dusty Pink there for when you come back to it) and knit to end of row.
Row 12: Purl the loopy yarn to end of row.
Row 13: Cut the loopy yarn leaving a long length to darn in later. Using Dusty Pink, knit to end of row.

Change to flat ribbing (in Dusty Pink) as follows:
Row 14: *K2, P2, repeat from * to end of row.
Row 15: *P2, slip 2 purlwise, repeat from * to end of row.
Repeat these last 2 rows a further 4 times (10 rows of ribbing in all).

Cast off normally, but loosely.

Make the Twirly Fascinator again using White Zarina, but do NOT change to the loopy yarn mid-stream.

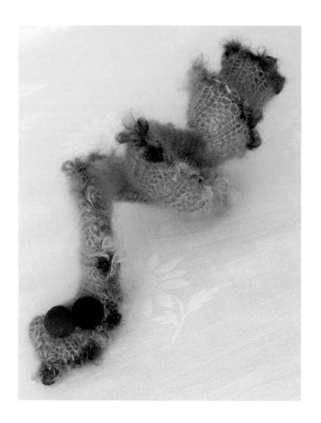

Sew the White Twirly Fascinator Lining together FIRST by sewing the cast-on edge to the cast-off edge to form a long tube. A simple tacking stitch from front to back should do it. Leave the ends open. Now stretch and sew the Dusty Pink Twirly Fascinator over the top leaving the ends open to insert the wire. Insert the bonsai wire into the plastic tubing and measure it against the fascinator band. Cut the plastic wire a bit longer than you need so that you can bend the ends over into a mini circle. You don't want it to poke through the knitting.

Insert the plastic-covered wire into the seam of the band (where the cast-off and cast-on edges have been sewn together) and secure it into place with some loose tacking stitches.

And again — the rest is up to you. Be game and pin before you sew. Oh, and add a couple of strategically placed felted balls.

Blue Beanie Beret

{KNITTED BERET}

People often tell me what great beanies One's tea cosies would make. If One was unkind, One would accuse People of starting the slow descent into la la land. MEN are wont to don tea cosies. It is how they show their affection for them and can be forgiven but One is a bit old fashioned. Beanies are for wearing and cosies are for warming tea.

It was while playing with the finished Blue Beanie Beret that the idea for the Spotted Gourd tea cosy grew. The old 'what if'.

Materials

* 2 x 50 g balls Debbie Bliss Donegal Luxury Tweed Aran: Real Blue
* Small amount Debbie Bliss Donegal Luxury Tweed Aran: Ice Blue

Equipment

* Two sets 5 mm (UK 6, USA 8) circular needles, 60 cm (24 in) long from needle tip to needle tip
* One pair 4 mm needles (UK 8, USA 6)

Method

Beanie knitted in the ROUND.
I prefer TWO SETS of circular
needles for this job (see page 12).
Rose knitted on the STRAIGHT.

Blue beanie beret

Using 5 mm (UK 6, USA 8) circular
needles and Real Blue, cast on
8 stitches and join in the round.

Work INCREASING rounds, as follows:
**Round 1 (and each alternate
round):** Knit.
Round 2: Increase by knitting into
the front and back of every stitch.
Round 4: *K1, increase in next stitch,
repeat from * to end of round.
Round 6: *K2, increase in next stitch,
repeat from * to end of round.
Round 8: *K3, increase in next stitch,
repeat from * to end of round.
Round 10: *K4, increase in next stitch,
repeat from * to end of round.
Continue in this increasing pattern
until there are 12 stitches in each
segment of the pie, 48 stitches on each
cable — a total of 96 stitches.

Keep increasing in the same manner
but with TWO rounds between each
increasing round until there are 16 stitches
in each segment of the pie, 64 stitches on
each cable — a total of 128 stitches.

Knit 2 rounds.

It is time to DECREASE. I'll get you started:
Round 1: *K14, K2tog, repeat
from * to end of round.
Knit two rounds.
Round 4: *K13, K2tog, repeat
from * to end of round.

Knit two rounds.
Round 7: *K12, K2tog, repeat from * to end of round.
Knit two rounds.
Round 10: *K11, K2tog, repeat from * to end of round.
Continue in this decreasing pattern — yes — with TWO rounds between each decreasing round, until there are 8 stitches in each segment of the pie, 32 stitches on each cable — a total of 64 stitches. Knit 16 rows without shaping and then cast off with Jeny's Surprisingly Elastic Bind-Off (see page 14).

Rose

Using 4 mm (UK 8, USA 6) needles and Ice Blue, cast on 28 stitches.
K1, P1 rib for 3 rows.

Row 4: Increase by knitting into the front and back of every stitch.
Row 5: Purl.
Row 6: Knit.
Work a further 4 rows in stocking stitch. Cast off in the usual fashion and not with the elastic version. It helps the rose to curl up nicely if the cast-off is reasonably tight. Twirl with the curl so that the wrong side of the stocking stitch faces up and out. Sew it in place at the base.

Putting it all together

You could stitch the Rose to the beret or tie it to a brooch pin so that you can be flowery or not, depending on your mood.

The Blue Scarf

{DOUBLE KNITTED SCARF}

A scarf in a tea cosy book? Well why not. There's a beanie beret! Unless you're already extremely clever, you can't just go knitting Willow (on page 84) or Gone Potty (on page 88) willy nilly without learning how to do Double Knitting first. So, if you have never done double knitting, this is a good, easy project to start with.

I reckon my instructions below are pretty good, but you can always Google YouTube for video instructions. The graphed pattern for the scarf is very simple and will give you a chance to get into the swing of the technique without having to concentrate too hard on an intricate graph.

Stop when you've had enough and whip on over to Willow or Gone Potty.

A short diversion while you learn to do double knitting

WHAT IS DOUBLE KNITTING?

Double knitting is a very clever technique where back-to-back fabrics are knitted simultaneously using two threads on ONE pair of needles. You get reversible knitting, double thickness with stocking stitch on both sides. Sound complicated? It is not. It is ingenious. I just want to knit everything in double knitting, that's when I'm not knitting everything in the round.

I discovered double knitting in Elizabeth Zimmerman's *Knitter's Almanac* but she does not lay claim to it. Now a technique cannot be copyrighted, but I wonder if it has been around too long to know who 'owns' it. I am astounded by the ability to even conceive of a new technique let alone sit down and work it out.

HOW TO DO DOUBLE KNITTING

You will be using two threads in two different colours (in the instructions below, I have used Blue and White). Ideally, you would knit with one colour in one hand and the other colour in the other hand. It goes really fast. It helps if you can knit both in the Continental style and in the Australian/English style, but it isn't absolutely necessary. I have seen knitters manage very comfortably holding the two different coloured yarns in the one hand.

WORKING THE DOUBLE KNITTING ROWS

You could (said grudgingly) use straight needles for this, but I use circular needles for everything, so why would you want to use anything else? Remember Mrs Frogmorton …

Cast on an ODD number of stitches in Blue.
Row 1: K2, *bring the yarn to the front and slip the next stitch purlwise, take the yarn to the back and K1, repeat from * to the last 3 stitches, slip 1 purlwise, K2.

Very Important Hint: To have a tight edge, knit the first Blue stitch then pull the working yarn downwards, tightening the stitch on the row below. Knit the next Blue stitch and do the same. Starting and finishing each row with K2 gives the knitting a neat garter stitch border on both edges.

Row 2: K2 (Blue), join in the White yarn, *take both yarns to the back, K1 with the White yarn only, bring both yarns to the front, P1 with the Blue yarn only, repeat from * to the last 3 stitches, take both yarns to the back, K1 with the WHITE yarn only, take both yarns to the back, K2 (Blue).
Row 3: K2 (Blue), *bring both yarns forward, P1 with the White yarn only, take both yarns to the back, K1 with the Blue yarn only, repeat from * to the last 3 stitches, bring both yarns forward, P1 with the White yarn only, K2 (Blue).
Row 4: K2 (Blue), *take both yarns to the back, K1 with the White yarn only, bring both yarns to the front, P1 with the Blue yarn only, repeat from

* to the last 3 stitches, take both yarns to the back, K1 (White), K2 (Blue).

EXTREMELY Important Hint: After knitting the first two Blue stitches of each row, twist the White and Blue threads around each other so that they catch before making the next stitch. If you don't do the thread twist, the White back and the Blue front (or vice versa) will not be joined together at the edge of the fabric. Pull the working yarn downwards on the first stitch of the double-sided knitting, to tighten the stitch on the row below.

If you have worked four rows and only just now read the Extremely Important Hint, don't fret. Just start doing the thread twist now. Not a soul will know. It will be our little secret.

You are on your way. All you have to do now is follow the pattern graphs. Two graphs? Yes, there are two graphs because when a double knit graph is not symmetrical, it is extremely hard to read and remember where you are up to. It is better to have the two graphs, one for when the Blue is the main/dominant/background colour facing you, and one for when the White is the background colour facing you. Count count and count.

Speaking of the end …

FINISHING OFF

You will see that on one side of the knitted fabric, the background colour goes all the way to the edge of the square. On the other side, the background colour is framed at each edge by a narrow border of contrasting colour. With this framed side facing you, you can prepare for casting off. But we are not actually casting off just yet. We are framing the top of the square before cast-off, to make it match nicely with the sides and bottom.

With the framed side facing you, ready to work, cut off the background colour yarn, leaving a long thread to darn in later. Using the 'frame' colour, knit the first 2 stitches as usual. Continuing in the 'frame' colour, *K1, bring the yarn to the front, slip the next stitch purlwise, take the yarn to the back, repeat from * to the last 3 stitches, take the yarn to the back, K3.

CASTING OFF

Now you will have the side facing where the background colour goes all the way to the edge of the square.

To cast off, K2, P1, lift the back 2 stitches over the front stitch and off the working needle, *K1, P1, lift the back 2 stitches over the front stitch and off the working needle, repeat from * to the end. Cut the yarn and tie off.

Using a crochet hook, whisk the loose ends down through the middle of the double-sided knitting, never to be seen again.

BACK TO THE BLUE SCARF…

Size

Approximately 22 cm wide x
50 cm long (7½ x 19½ in).

Materials

3 x 50 g (1¾ oz) balls Debbie Bliss
Donegal Luxury Tweed Aran: Ice Blue
3 x 50 g (1¾ oz) balls Debbie Bliss
Donegal Luxury Tweed Aran: Real Blue

Equipment

* One set 5 mm (UK 6, USA 8)
  circular needles, 80 cm (31½ in) long
  from needle tip to needle tip
* One set 4 mm (UK 8, USA 6)
  circular needles, 80 cm (31½ in) long
  from needle tip to needle tip
* Crochet hook for whisking away
  the loose threads at the end

Method

Double knitting: knitted on the STRAIGHT using circular needles.

Scarf

Using 4 mm (UK 8, USA 6) needles and Real Blue, cast on 73 stitches. (Remember, 2 are for the left edge, 2 are for the right edge and the remaining 69 stitches will divide themselves into front and back — 34 Real Blue and 35 Ice Blue.)

Change to 5 mm (UK 6, USA 8) needles.

Row 1: K2, *bring the yarn to the front and slip the next stitch purlwise, take the yarn to the back and K1, repeat from * to the last 3 stitches, slip 1 purlwise, K2.

Row 2: K2 (Real Blue), join in the Ice Blue yarn, *take both yarns to the back, K1 with the Ice Blue yarn only, bring both yarns to the front, P1 with the Real Blue yarn only, repeat from * to the last 3 stitches, take both yarns to the back, K1 with the Ice Blue yarn only, K2 (Real Blue).

Row 3: K2 (Real Blue), *bring both yarns forward, P1 with the Ice Blue yarn only, take both yarns to the back, K1 with the Real Blue yarn only, repeat from * to the last 3 stitches, bring both yarns forward, P1 with the Ice Blue yarn only, take both yarns to the back, K2 (Real Blue).

Row 4: K2 (Real Blue), *take both yarns to the back, K1 with the Ice Blue yarn only, bring both yarns to the front, P1 with the Real Blue yarn only, repeat from * to the last 3 stitches, take both yarns to the back, K1 (Ice Blue), K2 (Real Blue).

Continue to refer to Working the double knitting rows (on page 80) … at the same time as following the Blue Scarf graphs (see pages 142–143). You'll note that I have started you on your way with this graph but the rest is up to you. Make it up. Or turn it upside down. Or repeat it. It doesn't matter. Not one bit. It is yours to do with as you will.

When you've had enough, follow the instructions for Finishing off (on page 80). You double knitter, you.

Willow

{DOUBLE KNITTED TEA COSY}

For Kerrie of Quorrobolong (near Newcastle)

Methinks Kerrie is collecting tea cosy workshops. She has been to three of mine, but rather than freak out about having a stalker, I put her to work! Kerrie became one of my Three Fabulous Knitters for this book. I have never had Three Fabulous Knitters before. I have never had ANY knitters before. Besides knitting for me, Kerrie also knits tea cosies for auction at her annual local fire brigade fundraiser. When Kerrie isn't knitting or working, she plays with her dogs and her husband.

When you do tackle the Willow pattern, abstention from alcoholic beverages is strongly advised. Best to get some stitches under your belt first. You will deserve a full-bodied red at the end.

Size

Big. Oh OK. My Willow sides measure 24 cm (9½ in) high and 34 cm (13½ in) wide. That will keep one helluva big pot of tea warm.

Materials

* 2 x 50 g (1¾ oz) balls Debbie Bliss Donegal Luxury Tweed Aran: Real Blue
* 2 x 50 g (1¾ oz) balls Louisa Harding Thistle: Natural

Equipment

* One set 4 mm (UK 8, USA 6) circular needles, 80 cm (31½ in) long from needle tip to needle tip
* One set 5 mm (UK 6, USA 8) circular needles, 80 cm (31½ in) long from needle tip to needle tip
* Crochet hook for whisking away the loose threads at the end

Method

Double knitting: knitted on the STRAIGHT using circular needles.

Cosy front

Using 4 mm (UK 8, USA 6) needles and Real Blue yarn, cast on 99 stitches. Sounds like a lot of stitches doesn't it, but 2 are for the left edge, 2 are for the right edge and the remaining 95 stitches will divide themselves into front and back — 47 Blue and 48 Natural.

Change to 5 mm (UK 6, USA 8) needles.
Row 1: K2, *bring the yarn to the front and slip the next stitch purlwise, take the yarn to the back and K1, repeat from * to the last 3 stitches, slip 1 purlwise, K2.
Row 2: K2 (Real Blue), join in the Natural yarn, *take both yarns to the back, K1 with the Natural yarn only, bring both yarns to the front, P1 with the Real Blue yarn only, repeat from * to the last 3 stitches, take both yarns to the back, K1 with the Natural yarn only, K2 (Real Blue). Continue to refer to Working the double knitting rows (on page 80), at the same time as following Willow Large Pagoda graphs (on pages 144 and 145).

Cosy back

Work the Back in the same way as the Front, but following Willow Small Pagoda graphs (on pages 146 and 147).

Putting it all together

Using mattress stitch (see page 14), sew the Front and Back together, along the sides and top, leaving openings for the spout and handle. I also left the upper corners open. Work your mattress stitch neatly and the cosy will be completely reversible. How clever is that.

Gone Potty

{DOUBLE KNITTED TEA COSY}

For the CWA Wonder Women of Exeter

On a freezing cold October day in a small village in the Southern Highlands of New South Wales, the CWA Wonder Women of Exeter put on a show. There was a pipe band and heartfelt speeches and a fair dinkum* auction with a fair dinkum* auctioneer.

Pollies were present. A string quartet played. The sun stayed out. Tea and scones warmed the bellies and hearts of all the potty people there to buy 400 handmade tea cosies and raise $17,000 for cancer charity.

And what is the CWA, I hear you ask from abroad. It is the Country Women's Association, in action for regional communities since 1922. And a damn good job too.

*Fair Dinkum: Australian slang for 'real'. It is important to translate these things, to educate the world in the ways of those Down Under. Down Under: American slang for Australia. Oh yeah! And 'Pollies': Not as in 'Polly want a cracker' but as in 'Politician'.

Size

REALLY Big. Big like a CWA teapot big. My Gone Potty sides measure 24 cm (9½ in) high and 34 cm (13½ in) wide.

Materials

3 x 50 g (1¾ oz) balls Debbie Bliss Donegal Luxury Tweed Aran: Green
3 x 50 g (1¾ oz) balls Debbie Bliss Donegal Luxury Tweed Aran: Pink

Equipment

* One set 4 mm (UK 8, USA 6) circular needles, 80 cm (31½ in) long from needle tip to needle tip
* One set 5 mm (UK 6, USA 8) circular needles, 80 cm (31½ in) long from needle tip to needle tip
* Crochet hook for whisking away the loose threads at the end
* Pompom maker, 3.5 cm (1½ in) diameter

Cosy front

Using 4 mm (UK 8, USA 6) needles and
Green, cast on 103 stitches. (2 stitches are for
the left edge, 2 are for the right edge and the
remaining 99 stitches will divide themselves
into front and back — 49 Green and 50 Pink.)

Change to 5 mm (UK 6, USA 8) needles.
Row 1: K2, *bring the yarn to the front
and slip the next stitch purlwise, take the
yarn to the back and K1, repeat from *
to the last 3 stitches, slip 1 purlwise, K2.
Row 2: K2 (Green), join in the Pink
yarn, *take both yarns to the back, K1
with the Pink yarn only, bring both
yarns to the front, P1 with the Green
yarn only, repeat from * to the last
3 stitches, take both yarns to the back,
K1 with the Pink yarn only, K2 (Green).

Continue to refer to Working the
double knitting rows (see page 80),
at the same time as following Gone
Potty Teapot graphs (on pages 148
and 149). Don't drink and COUNT.

Cosy back

Work the Back in the same way as the
Front, but following Gone Potty Hearts
graphs (on pages 150 and 151).

Putting it all together

Make 10 pompoms. Three Green and Seven
Pink. Go on, it's fun. Leave long tails on
your pompoms. Place the Front and Back
together and catch in place at intervals
around the edge with a pair of pompoms.
That's why you left the long tails.

Spotted Gourd

{KNITTED AND FELTED TEA COSY}

For Pam of Bingara

*The more ideas you have, the more ideas you have. I made the
Blue Beanie Beret first and was playing with it on my lap,
folding it and moulding it and I said to myself, I said, what if I had
two of these and sewed them together along the crown and turned
it upside down and decreased the openings into gourd shapes and
stabilised it with a bit of bonsai wire and fluffed it up with feathers.
I said all that to myself, I did. And voilà! A tea cosy.*

*Spotted Gourd is for Pam who is as game as game in life and came
to my workshop at the Nundle Woollen Mill, thinking she would find
a little woolly respite but found she was expected to be as game
as game in knitting too. Pam being Pam ... well she was back
for more game respite the next year ... and the next.*

Size

To fit a four-cup teapot that stands 10 cm (4 in)
tall (not including the knob) and 12 cm (5 in) in
diameter (not including the spout and handle).

Materials

* 3 x 50 g (1¾ oz) balls Nundle
  Collection 8-ply wool: Aqua
* 2mm-diameter (⅛ in) bonsai wire
* Plastic tubing with inner diameter wide
  enough to insert the bonsai wire
* Small amount feltable white wool
* White feathers

Equipment

* Two sets 5 mm (UK 6, USA 8)
  circular needles, 60 cm (24 in)
  long from needle tip to needle tip
* Darning needle
* Scissors

Method

Knitted in the ROUND. I used TWO
SETS of circular needles (see page 12).

Gourd (make 2)

Using 5 mm (UK 6, USA 8) needles and
Aqua yarn, cast on 8 stitches. Join in the round.

Work INCREASING rounds, as follows:
**Round 1 (and each alternate
round):** Knit.
Round 2: Increase by knitting into
the front and back of every stitch.
Round 4: *K1, increase in next stitch,
repeat from * to end of round.
Round 6: *K2, increase in next stitch,
repeat from * to end of round.
Round 8: *K3, increase in next stitch,
repeat from * to end of round.
Round 10: *K4, increase in next stitch,
repeat from * to end of round.
Continue in this increasing pattern
until there are 12 stitches in each
segment of the pie, 48 stitches on each
cable — a total of 96 stitches.

Keep increasing in the same manner
but with TWO rounds between each

increasing round until there are 16 stitches in each segment of the pie, 64 stitches on each cable — a total of 128 stitches.

Knit 2 rounds.

It is time to DECREASE. I'll get you started:
Round 1: *K14, K2tog, repeat from * to end of round.
Knit two rounds.
Round 4: *K13, K2tog, repeat from * to end of round.
Knit two rounds.
Round 7: *K12, K2tog, repeat from * to end of round.
Knit two rounds.
Round 10: *K11, K2tog, repeat from * to end of round.
Knit two rounds.
Continue in this decreasing pattern until there are 6 stitches in each segment of the pie, 24 stitches on each cable — a total of 48 stitches.

Now follow the pattern — it changes and changes again:
Round 1: *K4, K2tog, repeat from * to end of round.
Knit two rounds.
Round 4: *K3, K2tog, repeat from * to end of round.
Knit FOUR rounds.

(Note. Knit five rounds when making the second gourd to make it slightly taller than the first.)

Round 9: *K2, K2tog, repeat from * to end of round.
Knit SIX rounds.

(Note. Knit seven rounds on the second gourd.)

There are now 12 stitches on each cable — a total of 24.
Round 16: *K4, K2tog, repeat from * to end of round.
Knit SIX rounds.

(Note. Knit seven rounds on the second gourd.)

Round 23: *K3, K2tog, repeat from * to end of round.
Knit SIX rounds.

(Note. Knit seven rounds on the second gourd.)

Round 30: *K2, K2tog, repeat from * to end of round.
Knit ONE round.

Increase for the little trumpet bell at the top, as follows:
Round 1: *K1, M1 (see page 15), K1, repeat from * to end of round.
Knit TWO rounds.

Round 4: *K1, M1, K2, repeat from * to end of round.
Knit TWO rounds.

Round 7: *K1, M1, K3, repeat from * to end of round.
Knit TWO rounds.
Round 10: *K1, M1, K4, repeat from * to end of round.
Knit SIX rounds.

Cast off.

Felting

Fold the bladders back in on themselves to form the two halves of the cosy. Sew them together along the bottom for about 9 cm (3½ in) on either side of the cast-on centre. Knot a couple of strands of white wool firmly to the outside of each half of the gourd in about eight or so places and trim the ends back to about 2 cm (1 in). Chuck the whole thing into a hot cycle in the washing machine, twice or thrice for a good old felting.

Putting it all together

Measure the perimeter of one of the gourds and add a few centimetres (or an inch or two) for luck. Easy to cut off extra. Impossible to add extra on. Cut a length of plastic tubing and a length of bonsai wire to measure. Thread the bonsai wire down the middle of the plastic tubing. Insert the protected wire down into the gourds, one for each, and work them out into the furthest reaches of the belly with the ends poking out the top of the trumpet bells. Mould the knitted fabric into a good shape before drying in the sun.

The rest is all window dressing. Choose your fluff well. A couple of fluffy white feathers did the job for me.

Oh yes, and you need a catch of some sort to hold the two standy-up bits together over the top of the teapot.

And what is that green thing doing over there? She is not related to Spotted Gourd but she is of the same species. An alien species but the SAME alien species. They are the same but different. Genes are a funny thing. One wonders what their offspring might look like. Mix it up girls. Mix it up.

Mediterranean Summer

{KNITTED AND FELTED TEA COSY}

For Joy of Adelaide

Joy! I always say I do … do it with love and Joy. Well I never knew who Joy was, I never did, until she wrote to me accusing me of all sorts of dreadful things, mostly for making her break her vow and declaration of thirty years to never knit again.

'I vowed and declared I would never knit again,' Joy wrote. 'It is all your fault,' she penned. 'I usually lead a very active life but I spent the whole weekend in my lounge chair, knitting.' And now she was looking for KA (Knitters Anonymous).

I said Joy, I said, there is no Knitters Anonymous but there are anonymous knitters and it is time you Come Out and KNIT over the world, you know, like TAKE over the world. Knit over the world with love and Joy? Get it Joy? Get it?

Size

To fit a three-cup teapot that stands just about as tall as you like and 12 cm (5 in) in diameter (not including the spout and handle). I hope you are not too attached, though, to the teapot you have chosen. My cosy felted so excellently that I had to find a new smaller pot. It is, after all, all about the cosy.

Materials

* 1 x 50 g (1¾ oz) ball Nundle Collection 8-ply wool, Main Colour (MC): Fern Green (see Note opposite)
* 1 x 50 g (1¾ oz) ball Nundle Collection 8-ply wool, Contrasting Colour (CC): Cerise
* Polyester fibrefill

Note. It is essential to use excellent felting wool for this cosy. The Nundle Collection 8-ply is perfect. If you can't get Nundle (it is available online), be sure to use a sturdy, old fashioned, earthy wool to give the tower that nice stand-up-on-your-own-ability.

Equipment

* Two sets 5 mm (UK 6, USA 8) circular needles, 60 cm (24 in) long from needle tip to needle tip
* Scissors
* Darning needle

Method

Knitted in the ROUND. I used TWO SETS of circular needles (see page 12).

Body

LOWER BODY

Remember you will be working ROUNDS and ROWS and things change.

Using both sets of 5 mm (UK 6, USA 8) circular needles and MC (Fern Green), cast on 80 stitches, 40 stitches on one set of needles and 40 stitches on the other set of needles.

Rounds 1–10: Purl.
Join in CC (Cerise).

Note. Even though the stripes are only 4 stitches wide, it would be wise to weave in the travelling yarn at the back as you go in the second or third stitch, in true Fair Isle fashion. And in true Fair Isle fashion, keep that travelling yarn loose at the back. You are not trying to create folds like those two rowdy dancing girls (see pages 102 and 108) like to wear.

Rounds 11–15: K4 (CC), K4 (MC).
Divide for sides as follows:

SIDE ONE

Now you will begin to work in ROWS not rounds. To start working rows, turn the work so that you are working back across the stitches you have just made.

Remember to make stocking stitch when working in ROWS: you will purl a row, then knit a row, purl a row, then knit a row.

Working in ROWS, continue the striped stocking stitch pattern up the first side of the tea cosy for 20 rows. Leave stitches on needle. Break off yarns, leaving a long length to darn in later.

SIDE TWO

With the wrong side facing you, join the yarn to the first stitch on the other circular needles and knit Side Two to correspond to Side One. Do NOT break off the yarns.

UPPER BODY

Join in the round again.
Knit 50 rounds continuing the striped stocking stitch pattern.

LID RIM

Break off CC, leaving a long end to darn in later. Knit one round in MC.
Purl 6 rounds in MC.
Break off MC, leaving a long end to darn in later.

LID

Join in CC.
Round 1: Knit to end of round.
Round 2: *K6, K2tog, repeat from * to end of round.
Round 3: Knit to end of round.
Round 4: *K5, K2tog, repeat

from * to end of round.

Round 5: Knit to end of round.

Round 6: *K4, K2tog, repeat from * to end of round.

Round 7: K5 (CC), join in MC, K5 (MC), *K5 (CC), K5 (MC), repeat from * to end of round.

Round 8: *[K3, K2tog] (CC), [K3, K2tog] (MC), repeat from * to end of round.

Round 9: *K4 (CC), K4 (MC), repeat from * to end of round.

Round 10: *[K2, K2tog] (CC), [K2, K2tog] (MC), repeat from * to end of round. Break off CC, leaving a long end to darn in later.

Round 11: Using MC only, knit to end of round.

Round 12: *K1, K2tog, repeat from * to end of round.

TOP POKEY UPPY BIT

Continue to knit the last 10 stitches in the round for 12 rounds.

If you have been knitting in the round on 2 sets of circular needles you might now use the Magic Loop method (see page 11) for this last bit. It is a bit less cumbersome on so few stitches. When you are done, break off the yarn and thread through those last 10 stitches. Draw the stitches tightly up together and darn the thread back down through Top Pokey Uppy Bit.

Lining

I didn't make a lining for this little fellow. I know. I know. But what is the point of making rules if you don't break them now and then? You be the judge. I felted him to within an inch of his life and all the important jobs of a cosy seemed to be taken care of.

Felting to within an inch of his life

I chucked him in the washing machine with normal washing powder and on the hot cycle and left him to it. He loved it so much he had three rides.

Stuffing

I have spread some fibrefill in the crown of the tower to help it spread and sit nicely. It should stay up there on its own, sticking a little to the felted fabric. You could also use stiff interfacing. Look at the instructions for Eugenie and Beatrice (on pages 69 and 73). And I have stuffed the bottom third of the tower just above the teapot. It is enough.

Betty the Burlesque Dancer

{KNITTED TEAPOT CORSET}

For Dawn

There are a lot of stitches in this little beauty. Betty is old school and expects the finest of fine in her finery. If you are in a hurry, you could use a thicker yarn and bigger needles with fewer stitches, but careful. Betty is no frump. Her beads were more expensive than the wool, for goodness sake, but she inSISTed on having them.

I met Pauline at a textile fair last year. She is a counsellor at a women's prison. Pauline took her knitting needles and wool and tea cosy books with her to work to start an inmates' Knit and Natter, Stitch and Bitch, Weave and Wag (chin wag that is). In the company of wool and needles and tea cosies, the women found a place to learn, teach, share, praise, laugh and create. Clever clever Pauline. And funny funny Dawn. I am told that Eddie Emu (Eddie is in Wild Tea Cosies*) has morphed into something rather raunchy in Dawn's knitting hands. Dawn, I hope you like Betty. She is for you and the women who keep your company. She is for the finest of the fine in all of us.*

Size

To fit a two-cup teapot that stands 9 cm (3½ in) tall (not including the knob) and 12 cm (4¾ in) in diameter (not including the spout and handle).

Materials

* 2 x 50 g (1¾ oz) balls Filatura di Crosa Zarina, Main Colour (MC): Chocolate Brown
* 3 x 50 g (1¾ oz) balls Filatura di Crosa Zarina, Contrast Colour (CC): Ruby Red (those buxom pompoms use a lot of wool)
* 28 classy pearl-and-gold beads

Equipment

* Two sets 2.75 mm (UK 12, USA 2) circular needles, 60 cm (24 in) long from needle tip to needle tip
* Scissors
* Darning needle
* Pompom maker, 7 cm (2¾ in) diameter

Method

Knitted in the ROUND from top to bottom. I used TWO SETS of circular needles (see page 12).

Cosy

LOWER CORSET
Remember you will be working in ROUNDS and ROWS and things change.

Using two sets of 2.75 mm (UK 12, USA 2) circular needles and MC (Chocolate Brown), cast on 140 stitches onto the first set of needles and 140 stitches onto the second set of needles. Join in the round, taking care that the stitches are not twisted around the needles.

Note. To make the clever pleats, pull the travelling yarn firmly across the back of the work to coax the previous group of 10 purl stitches into a fold. Yes, the wrong side of the stocking stitch is, in fact, the right side of the corset.

Round 1: Join in CC (Ruby Red). *CC yarn forward, P10 (CC), CC yarn back, MC yarn forward, P10 (MC), MC yarn

back, repeat from * to end of round.
Rounds 2–10: Continue in the same fashion, remembering to pull the travelling yarn firmly across the back to form the folds. Divide for sides as follows:

SIDE ONE

Now you will begin to work in ROWS, not rounds. To start working rows, turn the work so that you are working back across the stitches you have just made, beginning with a wrong side row. This is where two sets of circular needles come into their own. You will use only one set to work the rows of one side now, while the other set of circular needles acts as a stitch holder for the stitches waiting patiently on the other side.

Row 1 (wrong side): *MC yarn back, K10 (MC), MC yarn forward, CC yarn back, K10 (CC), CC yarn forward, repeat from * to end of row.

Note. Remember to twist the MC and the CC around each other at the beginning of every row to form the pleat at the edges.

Row 2: *CC yarn forward, P10 (CC), CC yarn back, MC yarn forward, P10 (MC), MC yarn back, repeat from * to end of round. Working in ROWS, continue the striped pleated pattern up the first side of the tea cosy for 25 rows in total. Leave stitches on needle. Break off yarn, leaving a long length to darn in later.

SIDE TWO

With the wrong side facing you, join MC (Chocolate Brown) to the first stitch on the other circular needles, knit 10 stitches, join in CC (Ruby Red) and knit 10 stitches. Work Side Two to correspond to Side One. Do NOT break off the yarns.

UPPER BODY

With the right side facing you, join to begin working in ROUNDS again. Work 24 rounds, continuing the striped pleated pattern as described in Rounds 1–10.
Round 25: Swap colours and work Chocolate Brown stitches over the Ruby Red stitches and work Ruby Red stitches over the Chocolate Brown stitches. Knit every stitch.
Rounds 26–29: *MC yarn forward, P10 (MC), MC yarn back, CC yarn forward, P10 (CC), MC yarn back, repeat from * to end of round.
Round 30: Break off CC, leaving a long end to darn in later. *K2tog, repeat from * to end of round.

Work Petite Picot Edge as follows:
Round 31: Knit.
Round 32: *yo, K2tog, repeat from * to end of round.
Round 33: *K1 into yo, K1, repeat from * to end of round.
Rounds 34–40: Knit.
Cast off.

Lining

TOP

Worked in ROUNDS from the top down.
Using 2.75 mm (UK 12, USA 2) circular
needles and CC (Ruby Red), cast
on 8 stitches. Join in the round.

**Round 1 (and each alternate
round):** Knit.
Round 2: Increase by knitting into
the front and back of every stitch.

Round 4: *K1, increase in next stitch,
repeat from * to end of round.
Round 6: *K2, increase in next stitch,
repeat from * to end of round.
Round 8: *K3, increase in next stitch,
repeat from * to end of round.
Continue in this increasing pattern until
there are 12 stitches in each segment
of the pie — a total of 96 stitches or
48 stitches on each set of needles.
Knit one round.

LINING SIDES

Worked in ROWS (not rounds). Work
back across the stitches you have just made,
starting with the wrong side facing you.
Row 1: Purl.
Row 2: *K1, P1, repeat
from * to end of row.
Row 3: *K1, P1, repeat
from * to end of row.
Repeat rows 2 and 3 until the ribbed
side measures long enough to cover
the bowl of the teapot just below the
handle and spout. Do not cast off.

Work the second side to match,
finishing with a right side row.

Join the work in the ROUND again. We
are now giving up the ribbed stitch, for
a stocking stitch, so knit 4 rounds.
   It is time for another fitting. Put the lining
on the pot. Place the outer corset on top.
Shjushj and moosh it all into place so that
the two line up nicely together. Now take
an educated guess as to how many more

rounds you will knit before it is time to work the picot edge. Keep fitting on your pot. The picot edge should peek out from below the outer corset and just touch the table.

Work Petite Picot Edge as follows:
Round 1: *yo, K2tog, repeat from * to end of round.
Round 2: *K1 into yo, K1, repeat from * to end of round. (You have now made the hemline.) Knit 9 rounds (or as many rounds as it takes to fold back under to almost meet the ribbing again).

Cast off with Jeny's Surprisingly Elastic Bind-Off (see page 14). Sew the hem up into place. You remember how to hem, yes? Go on. Yes you do.

Pompom bosoms

Make two large 7 cm-diameter (2¾ in) pompoms with the Ruby Red wool. Wind and wind lots of wool for two luscious thick pompom bosoms. Cut the tethering thread long so that pompoms can be easily secured to the dress. I always topiary my pompoms. Even with the most modern of modern pompom makers, a pompom will require trimming into shape with sharp scissors.

Putting it all together

Darn in all the ends.
If your beads are of the small delicate variety, they may need to be sewn on with needle and cotton thread. Hem the

neckline by folding the petite picot edging over and neatly stitch into place.

Put the corset on the teapot to find the natural position for the high 'waist'. It is OK to ride up the hem from the base of teapot a little bit, not too much. The frilly hem of the lining will peak out. Mark the waist line with pins, then undress Betty and use a darning needle with the Ruby Red yarn to gather in the bodice on the inside of the dress. Give Betty another fitting to be sure.

Turn the lining inside out and sew it to the inside of the corset with an easy tacking stitch around the spout and handle openings.

Place the pompom bosoms just so, and tether one to the inside left and one to the inside right of the dress. Place the dress on the teapot again. The cleavage may be gaping a bit, so make a couple of stitches at the centre front neckline hem and tether it to the centre back of the neckline hem.

Just like costume design.

Naughty Nancy

{KNITTED TEAPOT CORSET}

Nancy is Betty's twin sister (no, not identical). Nancy, like Betty, is no frump. You know how sisters can be. You might think she is the same as Betty but you'd be wrong. Yes Nancy's dress is much the same shape but the differences are in the knitting. Pink, red. Checks, stripes. Right side of stocking stitch, wrong side of stocking stitch. Petticoat, no petticoat. Beads, no beads. All these little things set them apart.

Size

To fit a two-cup teapot that stands 9 cm (3½ in) tall (not including the knob) and 12 cm (4¾ in) in diameter (not including the spout and handle).

Materials

* 3 x 50 g (1¾ oz) balls Filatura di Crosa Zarina, Main Colour (MC): Musk Stick
* 2 x 50 g (1¾ oz) balls Filatura di Crosa Zarina, Contrast Colour (CC): Charcoal

Equipment

* Two sets 2.75 mm (UK 12, USA 2) circular needles, 60 cm (24 in) long from needle tip to needle tip
* Scissors
* Darning needle
* Pompom maker, 7 cm (2¾ in) diameter

Method

Knitted in the ROUND from the bottom up. I used TWO SETS of circular needles for this job (see page 12).

Cosy

LOWER CORSET

Remember you will be working in ROUNDS and ROWS and things change.

Using 2.75 mm (UK 12, USA 2) circular needles and MC (Musk Stick), cast on 140 stitches onto the first needle set and 140 stitches onto the second needle set. Join in the round, taking care that the stitches are not twisted around the needles.

Note. To make the clever pleats, pull the travelling yarn firmly across the back of the work to coax the previous group of 10 knit stitches into a fold. Nancy's finery is knitted in stocking stitch with the right side facing. Just different enough from Betty's garb.

Round 1: Join in CC. *K10 (CC), K10 (MC), repeat from * to end of round.
Rounds 2–6: Repeat Round 1, remembering to pull the travelling yarn firmly across the back to form the folds.
Round 7: *K10 (MC), K10 (CC), repeat from * to end of round.
Rounds 8–12: Repeat round 7.

Divide for sides as follows:

SIDE ONE

Now you will begin to work in ROWS not rounds. To start working rows, turn the work so that you are working back across the stitches you have just made. This is where two sets of circular needles come into their own. You will use only one set to work the rows of one side now while the other set of circular needles acts as a stitch holder for the stitches waiting patiently on the other side.

Row 1: *P10 (MC), P10 (CC), repeat from * to end of row.

Note. Remember to twist the MC and the CC around each other at the beginning of every row to form the pleat at the edges.

Row 2: *K10 (CC), K10 (MC), repeat from * to end of round. Working in ROWS, continue the checked pleated pattern up the first side of the tea cosy for 30 rows in total. Leave stitches on needle. Break off yarn, leaving a long length to darn in later.

SIDE TWO

With the wrong side facing you, join MC (Musk Stick) to the first stitch on the other circular needles, purl 10 stitches. Join in CC and purl 10 stitches. Work Side Two to correspond to Side One. Do NOT break off the yarns.

UPPER BODY

Join to begin working in ROUNDS again. Work 24 rounds, continuing the checked pleated pattern as described in Rounds 1–12.

Round 25: Break off CC, leaving a long end to darn in later. Knit (MC) to end of round.
Round 26: *K2tog, repeat from * to end of round.
Round 27: Knit.

Work Petite Picot Edge as follows:
Round 28: *yo, K2tog, repeat from * to end of round.
Round 29: *K1 into yo, K1, repeat from * to end of round.
Rounds 30–36: Knit.
Cast off.

Lining

There is no lining for Nancy. It is still in the wash after dragging in the mud last night after a big night out on the town.

Pompom bosoms

Just as for Betty the Burlesque Dancer (see page 107).

Putting it all together

Talk to Betty — but Nancy is not really a beads girl. They cramp her style.

Isabella Cosy

{KNITTED AND FRILLED AND FELTED TEA COSY}

For Maree of Orange

So anyway, Maree wrote to me saying she had broken her leg and, well, what was a girl to do but knit every single tea cosy in Wild Tea Cosies *to keep her from going insane, but I reckon that, moving right along to lists of vintage tea cosy patterns and then her own creations — what are we up to now, about fifty cosies in the space of a few months? — she might already be insane, especially when you know she asked her long-suffering husband to make glass cabinets to house them all because she couldn't give them away AND they all have their own teapots to sit upon too.*

What do you think happened when REALLY Wild Tea Cosies *was published and without a broken limb for an excuse? There isn't anything to do with tea cosy nuts but to give them more tea cosies to knit and so Maree joined my Two Other Fabulous Knitters to become Three Fabulous Knitters for book three, so now when I say break a leg — careful.*

Size

To fit a six-cup teapot that stands 14 cm (5½ in) tall (not including the knob) and 14 cm (5½ in) in diameter (not including the spout and handle).

Materials

* 3 x 50 g (1¾ oz) balls Nundle Collection 8-ply wool, Main Colour (MC): Cerise (see Note opposite)
* 1 x 50 g (1¾ oz) ball Nundle 100% Mohair Loop, Contrast Colour (CC): Blue

Note. It is essential to use excellent felting wool for this cosy. The Nundle Collection 8-ply is perfect. If you can't get Nundle (it is available online), be sure to use a sturdy, old fashioned, earthy wool to give Queen Isabella that bit of extra je ne sais quoi. Well she IS European.

Equipment

* One pair or set 6 mm (UK 4, USA 10) needles — straight or circular, it doesn't matter
* Two sets 5 mm (UK 6, USA 8) circular needles, 100 cm (approximately 40 in) long from needle tip to needle tip
* About 15 felt balls in various sizes
* Scissors
* Darning needle

Method

Coat Front and Back knitted on the straight in ROWS.
Coat Frill knitted in the ROUND.
I used TWO SETS of circular needles for this job (see page 12).

Coat

Note. Back and Fronts are worked with a double strand of MC throughout.

BACK

Using 6 mm (UK 4, USA 10) needles and two strands of MC (Cerise), cast on 30 stitches.
Row 1: Knit.
Row 2: Purl.
Repeat these two rows a further 10 times (total 22 rows).

Begin decreasing as follows:

Note. The centre back decrease is more gradual than the shoulder decrease.

Row 23: K1, ssk, K24, K2tog, K1.
Row 24 (and each alternate row): Purl.
Row 25: K1, ssk, K9, K2tog, ssk, K9, K2tog, K1.
Row 27: K1, ssk, K18, K2tog, K1.
Row 29: K1, ssk, K6, K2tog, ssk, K6, K2tog, K1.
Row 31: K1, ssk, K12, K2tog, K1.
Row 33: K1, ssk, K3, K2tog, ssk, K3, K2tog, K1.
Row 35: K1, ssk, K6, K2tog, K1.
Row 36: Purl.
Cast off loosely knitwise.

LEFT FRONT

Using 6 mm (UK 4, USA 10) needles and two strands of MC, cast on 17 stitches.
Row 1: Knit.
Row 2: Purl.
Rows 3–22: Continue working in stocking stitch.
Row 23: K1, ssk, K14.
Row 24 (and each alternate row): Purl.
Row 25: K1, ssk, K13.
Row 27: K1, ssk, K12.
Row 29: K1, ssk, K11.
Row 31: K1, ssk, K7, K2tog, K1.
Row 33: K1, ssk, K5, K2tog, K1.
Row 35: K1, ssk, K3, K2tog, K1.
Row 36: Purl.
Cast off loosely knitwise.

RIGHT FRONT

Using 6 mm (UK 4, USA 10) needles and two strands of MC, cast on 17 stitches.
Row 1: Knit.

Row 2: Purl.
Rows 3–8: Continue working in stocking stitch.
Row 9: K2, yo twice, K2tog, knit to end of row.
Row 10: Purl to the double yo, purl once into the double yo, P2.
Row 11: K2, K1 into buttonhole, knit to end of row.
Rows 12–18: Continue working stocking stitch.
Row 19: K2, yo twice, K2tog, knit to end of row.
Row 20: Purl to the double yo, purl once into the double yo, P2.
Row 21: K2, K1 into buttonhole, knit to end of row.
Row 22 (and each alternate row): Purl.
Row 23: K14, K2tog, K1.
Row 25: K13, K2tog, K1.
Row 27: K12, K2tog, K1.
Row 29: K2, yo twice, K2tog, K7, K2tog, K1.
Row 30: Purl to the double yo, purl once into the double yo, P2.
Row 31: ssk, K1 into buttonhole, K7, K2tog, K1.
Row 32 (and each alternate row): Purl.
Row 33: K1, ssk, K5, K2tog, K1.
Row 35: K1, ssk, K3, K2tog, K1.
Row 36: Purl.
Cast off loosely knitwise.

JOINING FRONTS AND BACK

Now is the time to put it all together sans (that's French for 'without') the buttons. Remember, you are going to felt it to within an inch of its life and better that the beautiful buttons are not subjected to being crashed around a washing machine over and over.

Sew the Fronts and Back together at the decreasing edges and make a firm stitch or two at the hem line securing the two Fronts to the Back of the coat.

Frill

Time to pick up stitches for the Frill around the outside edges of the brunch coat. With the right side of the coat facing you, and starting at the Front hemline, use one strand of MC (Cerise) and one set of 5 mm

(UK 6, USA 8) circular needles to pick up 2 stitches for every double threaded stitch previously made on the 6 mm needles.

It is not important exactly how many stitches you pick up so don't be bothered with counting. All will be well. When you have finished picking up stitches along the bottom hemline, move all those stitches onto the cable of that set of circular needles, pick up the other set of 5 mm circular needles and continue picking up stitches around the Left Front edge, the neckline and the Right Front edge.

Note. DO NOT INCREASE along the Left Front vertical edge. DO NOT INCREASE along the Left Front bottom edge. Mark the beginning and end of this section with two strands of contrasting coloured wool so that you won't have to rely on your memory. This section is overlapped by the Right Front section. Everything will sit more plum WITHOUT a Frill on the Left Front.

Round 1: Knit.
Round 2: *K1, yarn forward, repeat from * to end of round.
Round 3 (and each alternate round): Knit into every knitted stitch. Knit into the BACK of every 'yarn forward' stitch.

Note. The point of the 'yarn forward' is to make a stitch, NOT to make a hole. If you preferred, you could make the extra stitches by knitting into the front and back of a stitch. It doesn't really matter. I took the yarn forward route thinking that it was faster and, as there would be a great deal of increasing and a lot of stitches to knit in the frill and that as it would all be felted into oblivion anyhow, that quicker was better.

Back to the pattern.
Round 4: *K2, yarn forward, repeat from * to end of round.
Round 6: *K3, yarn forward, repeat from * to end.
Round 8: *K4, yarn forward, repeat from * to end.
Round 9: Knit.
Break off MC, leaving a long end to darn in later.

Join in CC (Nundle Blue Mohair Loopy yarn).
Round 10: *K1, P1, repeat from * to end.
Cast off loosely knitwise.

Felting

Chuck it in the washing machine on a hot cycle with ordinary washing powder, two or three times. Smooth out to dry in the sun.

Putting it all together

Sew on the felt ball buttons and attach the Corsage. Easy peasy.
The only difference between Isabella Cosy and Isabella Teddy (showing off on the next page) is the placement of the armhole and the tossing-it-in-a-hot-wash for felting.

Felt ball corsage

I bought these little beauties and sewed them together randomly.

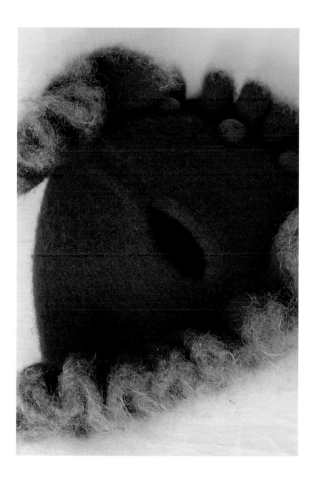

Isabella Teddy

{KNITTED AND FRILLED COAT FOR A TEDDY BEAR}

For Blue Ted

Jeni! Jeni! Look who I have for Blue Ted. Queen Isabella Teddy of the United Kingdom of Tedinous Bears. Isn't she gorgeous. No no I didn't knit Isabella. She hails from a knitting machine (I know, I know) in Lynmouth, Devon, England. I reckon she might have a bit of Spanish blood with a name like that. So what do you think? Is he up for it? Blue Ted?

Everything is just as for Isabella Cosy except for the sewing up part. Sew the straight sides together, leave the decreasing rows open for the teddy's arms and make a firm stitch or two at the neck line, securing the Left Front and the Right Front to the Back of the coat before you begin the frill.

Don't felt. Or felt. There is something very Aussie Brunch Coat about it not felted. All relaxed and homely. You could measure it up for your favourite little girl, though much bigger, and that Frill would be a challenge.

Unfelted, the tension (gauge) measures 20 rows x 14 stitches = 10 cm (4 in) square.

You'll find the pattern for the Rose on page 77.

Forest Bloom

{KNITTED COSY}

For Ali of Brisbane

Ali is not a knitter but it is my book and I get to name the cosies for whomever I will. Her story is not for these pages, but Ali is brave and loyal and clever and funny and beautiful and, well, thank goodness for Ali. Only a large and exuberant Forest Bloom will do for you, girl.

Size

To fit a six-cup teapot that stands 13 cm (5 in) tall (not including the knob) and 12 cm (4¾ in) in diameter (not including the spout and handle).

Materials

* 2 x 50 g (1¾ oz) balls Shelter (see Note below)
* 1 x 50 g (1¾ oz) ball Jo Sharp Silkroad Aran Tweed: Russet
* Yellow yarn for the centre pompoms

Note. I used three balls of Shelter, to get three different colours: Sap, Tent, and Button Jar. For the brown, any Aran tweed would be fine. For the yellow, I used a 4-ply (fingering weight) hand-dyed yarn and a bit of Moda Vera merino mohair blend in Mustard.

Equipment

* One set 4 mm (UK 8, USA 6) circular needles, 80 cm (31½ in) long from needle tip to needle tip
* One set 5 mm (UK 6, USA 8) circular needles, 80 cm (31½ in) long from needle tip to needle tip
* Darning needle
* Scissors
* Pompom maker, 3.5 cm (1½ in) diameter

Method

Petals knitted in the ROUND. I used the Magic Loop method for this job (see page 11). Body knitted in the ROUND. I used TWO sets of circular needles (see page 12).

Petals (make 5 for each bloom)

Using 4 mm (UK 8, USA 6) circular needles and Shelter yarn, cast on 8 stitches. Join in the round and follow the instructions for the Petals under **Egg Daisies**, on page 54. I made 5 Blooms and each Bloom has 5 Petals — so, 25 Petals in all.

FINISHING THE PETALS

Stretch and spread the petals into shape. The column of increases and decreases forms the centre vein of the petal. The two columns of purl stitches form the outside edges of the petal. Line up the petal veins front and back. Thread the long yarn end onto a darning needle and secure the front vein to the back vein with a simple tacking stitch, checking all the while that the veins are lined up exactly.

Using a steam iron on wool temperature, iron from the base of the petal (the fatter end) up towards the pointy bit. Hold the very tip of the petal while you iron upwards to help stretch it out long.

Body/lining (make 2)

Definitely make the Lining as well as the Body. Five large blooms atop will need some stability.

Using 5 mm (UK 6, USA 8) circular needles and Jo Sharp Silkroad Aran Tweed, cast on 8 stitches and join in the round. Proceed as for the **Basic Tea Cosy**, on page 16.

Putting it all together

Simple dimple. You need to construct the Blooms first. The short fat ends of the petals meet at the centre of the Bloom. Layering one short fat end over another short fat end, pin five Petals into a flower shape. You want to form a bowl rather than a flat mat. Start at the top of the first two short fat ends with an overstitch. Make a secret tacking stitch down the short fat ends, to not quite half

way, by sewing the bottom part of the top petal to the top part of the bottom petal. Join the other three petals in the same way.

Now make the pompoms and tie a pompom to the centre of each Bloom.

Make five big, beautiful Blooms.

Try your Blooms first atop the cosy Body. Try them again. Sew one into place. Try them all. Try them all again. Sew the next one into place. Try them all again. You get the picture. Isn't she just full of life! I love her.

Starry Night

{KNITTED COSY}

For the Wonderful Workshop Women

When one has a book, it is generally assumed by the great unwashed that one must know what One is talking about, or writing about, or knitting. Or more to the point, it is assumed that One must be able to TEACH it. And so the invitations come.

Well thank you, Oh Great Unwashed, because what a treat it is to share a few days with you, teaching and learning, always learning. You are not unwashed at all, but independent, clever, often working women, sneaking annual leave or flex days. You have organised care for husbands and children, sometimes travelled quite a distance and paid very good money just to play tea cosy with me. And you bring with you your child at heart, your joie de vivre. What a treat you are, Oh Wonderful Workshop Women.

Starry Night is for you because, after the frustrations of Devilish, and learning a whole new technique so that I could make some damned horns, I fell in love with short rows and secret wraps and bendy cones and I am reminded of being a student and of how hard and grand it can be too.

Size

To fit a six-cup teapot that stands 13 cm
(5 in) tall (not including the knob) and 12 cm
(4¾ in) in diameter (not including the spout
and handle). The best-shaped teapot for Starry
Night is something very round like a ball.

Materials

* 2 x 50 g (1¾ oz) balls Noro Kureyon, mostly
  Blue, for the Outer Cosy (see Note below)
* 1 x 50 g (1¾ oz) ball soft 8-ply
  wool, for the Cosy Lining

*Note. There is just slightly more than one 50 g
(1¾ oz) ball of wool in the Outer Cosy, but I
worked from 3 balls so that I could manage the
colours the way I wanted in the Starry Peaks.*

Equipment

* One set 5 mm (UK 6, USA 8) circular needles, 60 cm (24 in) from needle tip to needle tip
* Two sets 4 mm (UK 8, USA 6) circular needles, 80 cm (31½ in) long from needle tip to needle tip
* Polyester fibrefill
* Scissors
* Darning needle

Method

Starry Peaks knitted in the ROUND, using the Magic Loop method (see page 11). The Starry Peaks also feature Short Rows. Have a very good read of **About Short Rows** for Devilish on page 42. You will find an explanation of 'W&T' and 'PUwrap K2tog tbl' there too.

Cosy Front and Back, and the joining together of the Starry Peaks: all knitted on the straight. (I used circular needles.)

Ribbed Body knitted in the ROUND, using the Magic Loop.

Another abbreviation

M1 = Make 1 (see page 15).

Starry peaks (make 5)

Using 5 mm (UK 6, USA 8) circular needles and Noro Kureyon, cast on 6 stitches.
Rounds 1 & 2: Knit.
Round 3: (K1, M1, K2) twice.
Round 4: (K3, M1, K1) twice.
Round 5: (K1, M1, K4) twice (12 sts).
Rounds 6–8: Knit.

Very Important Note. Mark the beginning of the round with a contrasting coloured tie. It helps keep confusion at bay. I need all the help I can get. You might too.

Round 9: K1, W&T knitwise, P8, W&T purlwise, knit to end of round.
Round 10: K1, PUwrap K2tog tbl, K2, PUwrap K2tog tbl, knit to end of round.
Round 11: Knit.

Round 12: *K1, M1, K1, repeat from * to end of round.
Rounds 13–15: Knit.

Round 16: K2, W&T knitwise, P13, W&T purlwise, knit to end of round.
Round 17: K2, PUwrap K2tog tbl, K3, PUwrap K2tog tbl, knit to end of round.
Round 18: Knit.
Round 19: *K1, M1, K2, repeat from * to end of round.
Rounds 20–22: Knit.

Round 23: K3, W&T knitwise, P18, W&T purlwise, knit to end of round.
Round 24: K3, PUwrap K2tog tbl, K4, PUwrap K2tog tbl, knit to end of round.
Round 25: Knit.
Round 26: *K1, M1, K3, repeat from * to cnd of round.
Rounds 27–29: Knit.

Round 30: K4, W&T knitwise, P23, W&T purlwise, knit to end of round.
Round 31: K4, PUwrap K2tog tbl, K5, PUwrap K2tog tbl, knit to end of round.
Round 32: Knit.

The Last Round of the Starry Peak:
K13, cast off the next 4 stitches (there will now be 1 stitch on your working needle after the cast off section); K10, cast off the next 4 stitches (there should be 11 stitches left between each of the cast-off sections).

Move the first Starry Peak to two sets of 4 mm (UK 8, USA 6) circular needles, one set for the front stitches and one set for the back stitches. Put it aside and begin the next Starry Peak.

Place each of the completed Starry Peaks onto the same sets of waiting circular needles.

Joining the starry peaks

With all the concave fronts of the Starry Peaks facing and using one set of 5 mm (UK 6, USA 8) circular needles, you will now work back and forth in rows.

Row 1: Knit.
Row 2: Knit.

Note. There may be a very loose thread between the last stitch of a peak and the first stitch of the next peak. Pick that joining thread up and put it on the waiting needle then knit it together with the next proper stitch. This will firm up the join between the peaks.

Row 3: Purl.
Row 4: Knit.
Row 5: Purl.
Row 6: K9, *ssk, K2tog, K7, repeat from * twice more, ssk, K2tog, K9.
Rows 7–9: Continue in stocking stitch.
Row 10: K8, *ssk, K2tog, K5, repeat from * twice more, ssk, K2tog, K8.
Rows 11–13: Continue in stocking stitch.
Row 14: K7, *ssk, K2tog, K3, repeat from * twice more, ssk, K2tog, K7.
Knit 5 rows.
Cast off using Jeny's Surprisingly Elastic Bind-Off (see page 14).

With all the convex backs of the Starry Peaks facing you, repeat as for the front.

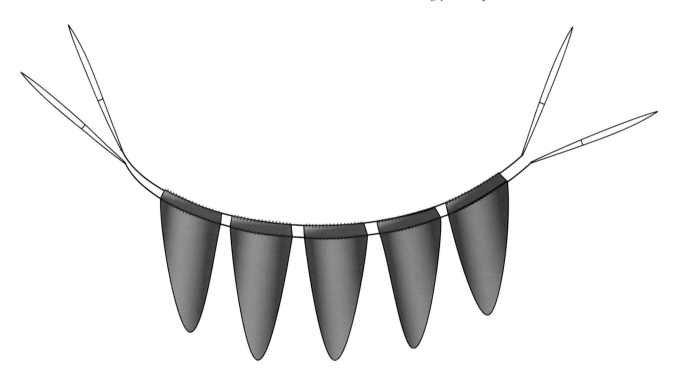

Now is a good time to sew the peaks together across the short cast-off edges using mattress stitch (see page 14).

Join the bottom front together, just under the spout, with a couple of stitches and join the bottom back together, just under the handle, with a couple of stitches.

Ribbed body

I called it the Ribbed Body but, hey and heck, it starts with the reverse side of stocking stitch. The Reverse Side of Stocking Stitch And Then The Ribbed Body was just too long a heading for my little old liking.

So anyway, with the right side facing and using 5 mm (UK 6, USA 8) circular needles, pick up approximately 70 stitches around the bottom of the cosy. Just be sure there is an even number of stitches for when you get to the ribbing.

Round 1: Knit.
Round 2: Purl.
Round 3: Purl (trust me).
Round 4: Purl.
Round 5: Knit.
Round 6: *K1, P1, repeat from * to end of round.

Now is a very good time to try it on your teapot. Hopefully you have tried it on a plethora of times already if only to see how fantastic it will look. Try it on now for length and continue knitting in the ribbed pattern until you think it is long enough. I needed another four rounds like this …

Rounds 7–10: Continue the 1x1 ribbing pattern. Cast off loosely.

Lining

Using 5 mm (UK 6, USA 8) circular needles and 8-ply wool, cast on 8 stitches. Proceed as for the **Basic Tea Cosy** on page 16.

Putting it all together

Fill the Starry Peaks with fibrefill but not too tightly. Mould the filling to accentuate the concave and convex arcs of the peak. You don't want to lose the effect of all that short row nonsense because of a bit of bad stuffing.

Gone Feral

{KNITTED TEA COSY}

There is that Manx Loaghtan again. Once something to be shy of,
a boring grey brown thing, not soft. And now I can't get enough of it.
Here it is in its obvious incarnation — something earthy, tribal, feral.
That poor old yak (I know, I know, he's really a sheep). He's probably
as tame as a … as tame as a … He's probably a very tame fellow.

Size

Make him as big as you like or as big as until
you get sick of knitting. Oooh that might be
never. It could be a knitted VW Beetle cover.

Materials

OUTER COSY (KNITTED)

* 2 x 100 g (3½ oz) balls Manx Loaghtan,
  Aran weight (see Note below)
* 1 x 50 g (1¾ oz) ball Noro
  Kureyon, for the fringe
* Small amount contrast yarn, for embroidery
* Feathers, lots of feathers,
  especially peacock feathers
* One big leather button

Note. This is a thicker Manx Loaghtan yarn than
the one used for the Bigs (Cosy and Bag), cos this
one comes all the way from the Isle of Man.

COSY LINING (SEWN)

* 80 x 80 cm (31½ x 31½ in) cotton print fabric
* 80 x 80 cm (31½ x 31½ in) one-sided iron-on
  stiff interfacing, plus a little extra for collage
* Sewing needle and cotton thread
  to match cotton print fabric
* Large piece of paper (newspaper
  will do), for template

Equipment

* One set 6 mm (UK 4, USA 10)
  circular needles, 80 cm (31½ in) long
  from needle tip to needle tip
* Darning needle
* Crochet hook, for fringe
* Pins
* Scissors
* Craft glue

1 Knit both Half-Moon Sides.
2 Embroider the contrast stitching.
3 Block both Sides. Definitely
   block the Sides.
4 Knit the Gusset to the length
   of the outside arc.
5 Make a paper template for the lining.
6 Cut and sew the lining.
7 Join the knitted Sides to
   the knitted Gusset.
8 Insert the cotton lining into the knitted
   cosy and stitch it all together.
9 Attach the Fringe.
10 Go wild with feathers.

Half-moon sides (make 2)

Using 6 mm (UK 4, USA 10) needles and
Manx Loaghtan, cast on 8 stitches. (That is
2 stitches for each end of the semi circle and
4 for the repeating increasing pattern.)

Row 1: Purl.
Row 2: K2, increase into front
and back of next 4 stitches, K2.
Row 3: Purl.

There is now a change in the way you increase.
Instead of knitting into the front and back
of a stitch, you will M1 (see page 15).

Row 4: K2, *K1, M1, K1, repeat
from * to last 2 stitches, K2.
Row 5: Purl.

Row 6: K2, *K1, M1, P1, M1, K1,
repeat from * to last 2 stitches, K2.
Row 7: P2, *P1, K3, P1, repeat

Method

Sides knitted on the STRAIGHT with circular
needles. Rim knitted on the STRAIGHT
with circular needles. Circular needles knit
around bends better. They do. They do.

Order — the all-important order

As with those beautiful Big French
Bags, the order in which you make
the parts is très important.

from * to the last 2 stitches, P2.
Row 8: K2, *K1, P3, K1, repeat
from * to the last 2 stitches, K2.
Row 9: P2, *P1, K3, P1, repeat
from * to the last 2 stitches, P2.

Row 10: K2* K1, M1, P3, M1, K1,
repeat from * to the last 2 stitches, K2.
Row 11: P2, *P1, K5, P1, repeat
from * to the last 2 stitches, P2.
Row 12: K2, *K1, P5, K1, repeat
from * to the last 2 stitches, K2.
Row 13: P2, *P1, K5, P1, repeat
from * to the last 2 stitches, P2.

Row 14: K2, *K1, M1, P5, M1, K1,
repeat from * to the last 2 stitches, K2.
Row 15: P2, *P1, K7, P1, repeat
from * to the last 2 stitches, P2.
Row 16: K2, *K1, P7, K1, repeat
from * to the last 2 stitches, K2.
Row 17: P2, *P1, K7, P1, repeat
from * to the last 2 stitches, P2.

Row 18: K2, *K1, M1, P7, M1, K1,
repeat from * to the last 2 stitches, K2.
Row 19: P2, *P1, K9, P1, repeat
from * to the last 2 stitches, P2.
Row 20: K2, *K1, P9, K1, repeat
from * to the last 2 stitches, K2.
Row 21: P2, *P1, K9, P1, repeat
from * to the last 2 stitches, P2.

Row 22: K2, *K1, M1, P9, M1, K1,
repeat from * to the last 2 stitches, K2.
Row 23: P2, *P1, K11, P1, repeat
from * to the last 2 stitches, P2.
Row 24: K2, *K1, P11, K1, repeat

from * to the last 2 stitches, K2.
Row 25: P2, *P1, K11, P1, repeat
from * to the last 2 stitches, P2.

Continue in this same increasing pattern until
the work measures 20 cm (8 in) or thereabouts.
Measure from the centre of the cast-on row
up the middle of the work, not along the
edge as the edge might be a little stretched.

Cast off with Jeny's Surprisingly
Elastic Bind-Off (see page 14).

Embroidery

Using contrast yarn, work a line of knitting stitch Vs, down each of the vertical ribs on each Side, and around the lower edge.

Blocking

Do not be tempted to skip this step. Wet the knitted Sides and spread on a towel on the verandah. Pat each one out into a beautiful symmetrical flat thing. Leave to dry.

Gusset

The Gusset is the knitted strip that keeps the Sides apart so that the cosy will sit nicely on top of your teapot. You should only knit it when you have blocked the Sides (you didn't skip that step, did you?), because the measurements need to be precise.

Using 6 mm (UK 4, USA 10) needles and Manx Loaghtan wool, cast on 10 stitches.
Row 1: K2, slip 2 purlwise (keeping the yarn at the back), K2, slip 2 purlwise (yarn at back), K2.
Row 2: P2, K2, P2, K2, P2.
Repeat these 2 rows until work measures the length of the outer arc of the blocked knitted Sides. Measure that outer arc once and twice and even thrice to be sure.

Fabric lining

Now you need to make a fabric lining for your cosy. I've said it all before, so go to Le Grand Sac à Main (on pages 36–37) and follow the instructions for making paper templates of the Side and Gusset, and stitching a fabric lining. Then bring it back here.

Putting it all together

With right sides together, join one knitted Side to the knitted Gusset with pins. Using a darning needle and Manx wool, sew the parts together using the simplest tacking stitch. Repeat for the second Side. Insert the fabric lining — wrong sides together — and sew it into place. This might not seem the best time to do this, but you need the strength of the lining with its stiff interfacing to hold the weight of the feather and button collage.

THE FRINGE

Use a crochet hook and lengths of Noro Kureyon to loop and knot the fringe through the edge of the Gusset. Of COURSE you know how to do this — push your crochet hook through the knitted fabric, pick up the loop on a doubled length of wool, draw it through the knitted fabric, pull the ends through the loop and pull firmly to knot it in place. Don't make the yarn lengths too long — you want your fringe to stand straight up, like a Mohawk punk hair-do.

GO WILD WITH FEATHERS

No, I am not going to tell you EXACTLY how to do this, because it's your cosy. Use the palette. Play. Arrange. Change. Leave. Play again. Pin.

When you have arrived at a truce with
your feathers, sew the larger ones,
such as the peacock feathers, directly
onto the cosy with cotton thread.
To keep control of your smaller feathers,
cut a half-moon shape of stiff interfacing
with a radius of about 4 cm (1½ in). Secure
a splay of feathers to the interfacing
shape with a little bit of craft glue.

Now you can secure the large leather button
to the half-moon of chicken feathers and
then to the cosy in one fell swoop. You will
need a strong sharp needle and thread. Put
extra stitches wherever you think you need
extra stitches to hold it all firmly in place.

Be GAME. It is all yours.
Go FERAL.

The 'Armless Brothers

{IDENTICAL TWIN KNITTED TEA COSIES}

For all the Men Who Have Trouble Parting With Their Favourite Jumpers

If you think these two look about as Australian as a pair of Afghans, well, you'd be right. We come in all shapes and sizes, creeds and colours, over here. And anyway, Australian is as Australian does.

Abdul and Faiz, descendants of the original Afghan cameleers, have occasionally been seen flirting with Betty and Nancy on a Friday night up at the local, but only when the footy isn't on the telly. Or the cricket. Or the tennis. Or the golf. So not often really. Silly old buggers.

Size

This is one of those that you might have to match the teapot to the cosy.

Materials

*   Abdul's old woollen jumper
*   3 x 50 g (1¾ oz) balls Naturally Aran Tweed (yummy New Zealand wool, hmmm mmmm) in a colour to match or contrast with your jumper
*   Polyester fibrefill
*   Decorative things that these old geezers might want to wear — a tassel, a pompom, a row of medals (YOU know what they're like)

Equipment

*   Two sets 5 mm (UK 6, USA 8) circular needles, 80 cm (31½ in) long from needletip to needletip
*   Scissors
*   Darning needle
*   Crochet hook small enough to get through the felted jumper but big enough to pick up the Aran wool

Method

Aran Rims and Cosy Lining knitted in the ROUND. I used TWO sets of circular needles (see page 12).

Outer cosy

FELTING

Felt the jumper first. Felt it again. And if you think it needs it, felt it again. Now it should be safe to cut with scissors without the stitches running out of control.

CUTTING AND FITTING

Cut the sleeves off the jumper close to the shoulder.

Now might be a good time to find the right sized teapot. Keep the teapot in front of you at all times and try on and try on throughout the making of the cosy.

The sleeve seam will mark the back of the tea cosy, the bit that will line up with the handle of the teapot.

Cut the back seam, very close in, either side of the seam, and snip and whip it away. Try it on the teapot. Cut up the imaginary front seam in a straight line exactly opposite the back seam opening. Try it on the teapot. Remember, you will have a lining on the pot so it will sit more snugly when that is made.

PICKING UP STITCHES ON CUT EDGES

With the right side facing and starting at the crux of the V cut for the handle (at the back), use the crochet hook to pick up stitches evenly around the opening. Pick up the stitches close to the edge but not so close as to unravel the knitted jumper. Bring 4 or 5 stitches through to the right side and then put those stitches onto the knitting needle (see photo opposite). Keep picking up stitches all the way around. Be conscious of the number of stitches you pick up along one edge and try to closely approximate that number of stitches along the corresponding edge.

VERY CLEVER RIM AROUND BOTTOM EDGES

Round 1: Purl (the wrong side of stocking stitch is the right side of the cosy).
Round 2: Purl to the corner and increase into the stitch before the corner and increase into the stitch after the corner. (Increase by knitting into the front and back of the stitch.)

Note. Increase, in this manner, at the corners and decrease at the crux of the Vs by knitting two stitches together just before the crux and immediately after the crux.

Round 3: Purl.
Round 4: Purl, increasing at the corners and decreasing at the crux.
Round 5: Purl.

Now this is the Very Clever bit. You want the rim to curl under snugly, so simply reverse the decreasing and increasing. Decrease at the corners and increase at the crux of the V.

Round 6: Purl, decreasing at the corners and increasing at the crux of the V.
Round 7: Purl.
Round 8: Purl, decreasing at the corners and increasing at the crux of the V.
Cast off loosely.

Fold the Very Clever Rim under and sew into place with a simple tacking stitch.

VERY CLEVER RIM AROUND TOP

Start out just as for the Very Clever Rim Around Bottom Edges, picking up stitches through the knitted fabric. It is preferable, but not imperative, to pick up a multiple of 4 stitches on one set of circular needles and also on the other set of circular needles. I picked up 28 + 28 (total 56) stitches around the top rim.

Rounds 1– 5: With the right side facing, purl.
Round 6: Knit.
Round 7: *K5, K2tog, repeat from * to end of round.
Round 8: Knit.
Round 9: *K4, K2tog, repeat from * to end of round.

Round 10: Knit.
Rounds 11–15: Purl.
Round 16: Knit.
Round 17: *K3, K2tog, repeat from * to end of round.
Round 18: Knit.
Round 19: *K2, K2tog, repeat from * to end of round.
Round 20: Knit.
Rounds 21–25: Purl.
Round 26: Knit.
Do NOT cast off. Cut off the yarn leaving a long end. Draw the long end through the remaining stitches and tie off.

Cosy lining

Using 5 mm (UK 6, USA 8) circular needles and Aran Tweed yarn, cast on 8 stitches. Proceed as for **Basic Tea Cosy** on page 16.

Putting it all together

Tack the Cosy Lining to the Outer Cosy around the front spout opening and a little way along each side. Leave the back flaps to do as they will. A little stitch at the crux of the V above the handle might not go astray. Fill with fibrefill, a little or a lot, and fold the sleeve or don't.

Add a tassel, a button, a pompom, a feather or all of the above and Bob's your uncle. Or rather, Abdul's your uncle. And so is Faiz. Now make his twin. Yes you can. Yes you will. They are TWIN tea cosies and one is not happy without the other.

Graphs

Graphs graphs graphs graphs, sung to the tune of the Mickey Mouse Club song, just to get you in a jolly mood. If you have never followed a graph before, don't be shy, they don't bite. You might even fall in love and want to knit everything from graphs — stitches and pictures.

Stitches and pictures? Well the Double Knitting graphs are just picture graphs, colour plans. The stitch graph belongs to Le Grand Sac à Main and to Le Grand Couvre-théière, and describes what stitch to use when, knit or purl, and when to increase. Follow the legend. Gorn (Aussie for 'go on')! You can do it.

The Blue Scarf

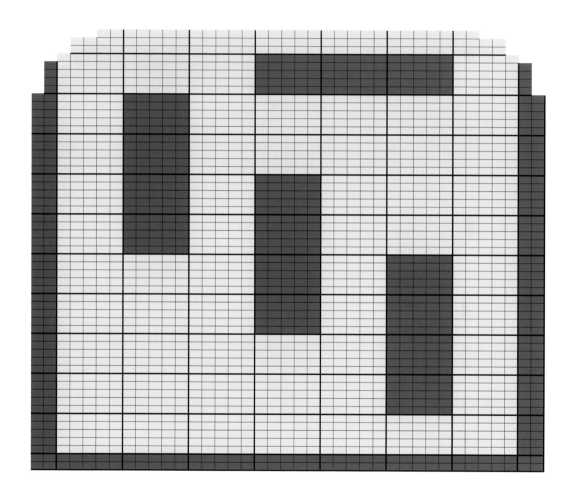

The Blue Scarf

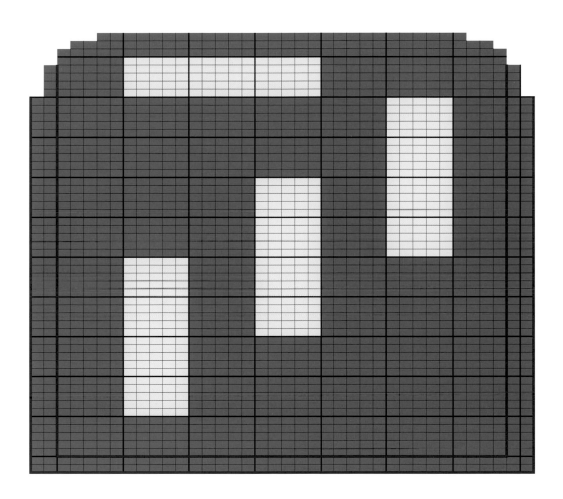

Willow

Willow

Willow

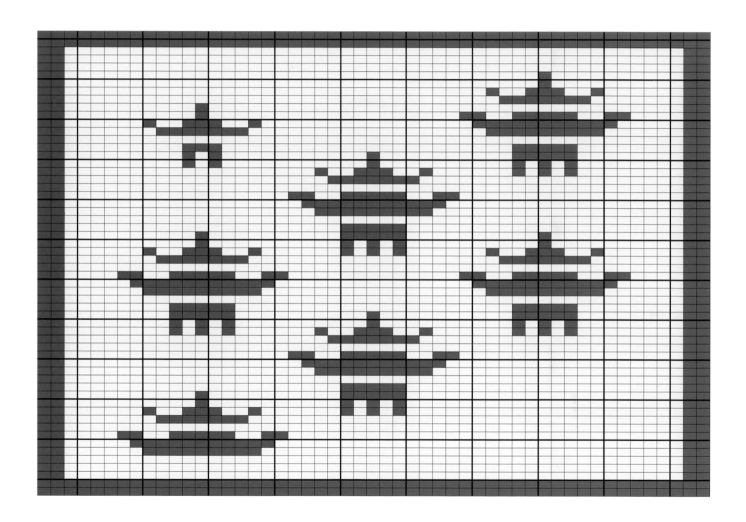

Willow

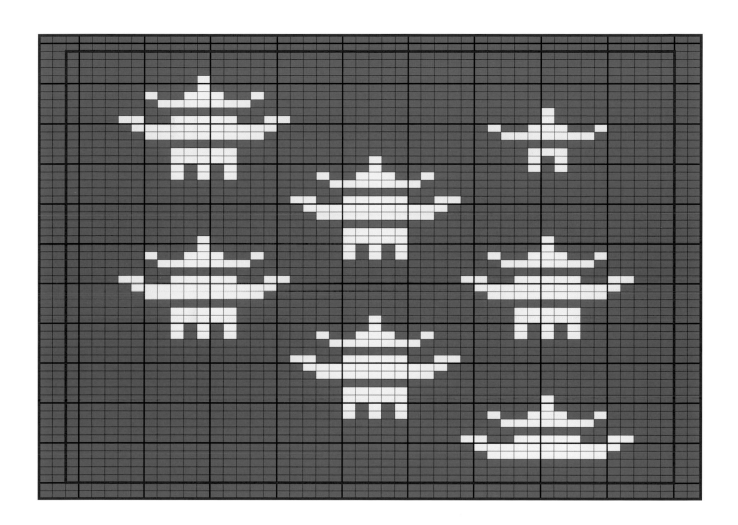

Gone Potty

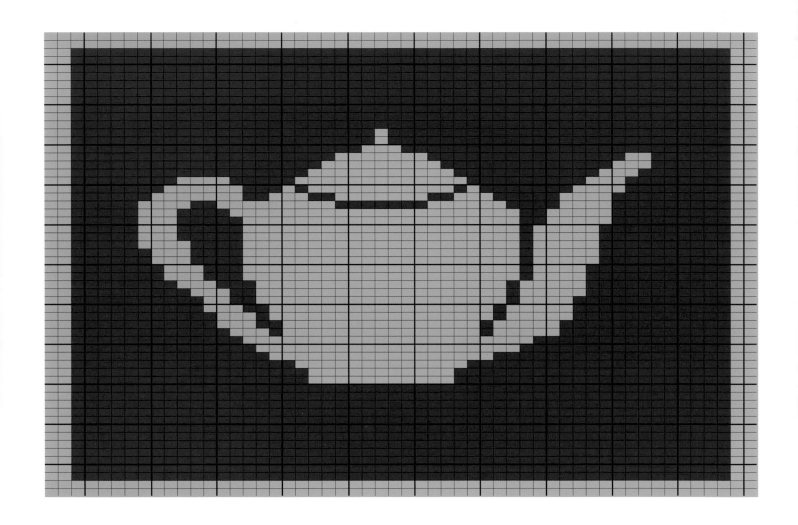

Gone Potty

Gone Potty

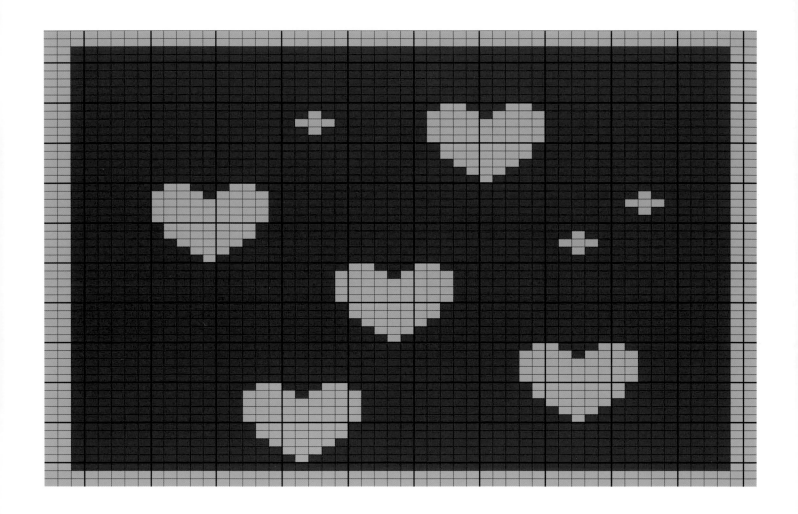

Gone Potty

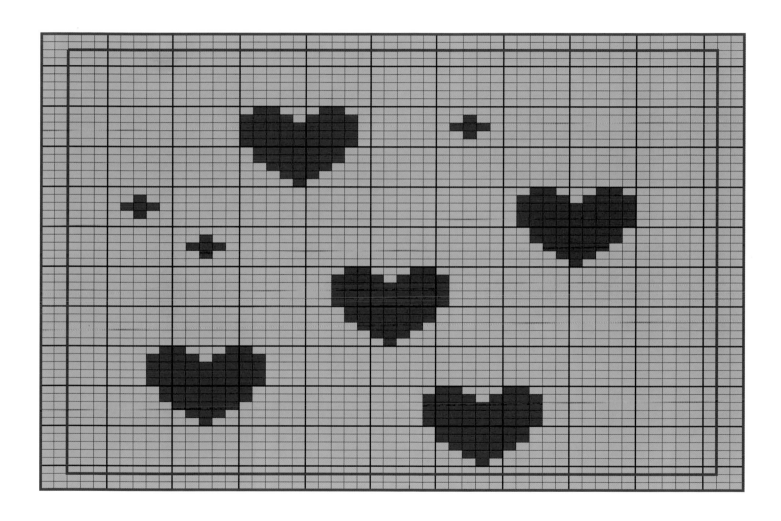

Le Grand Sac à Main

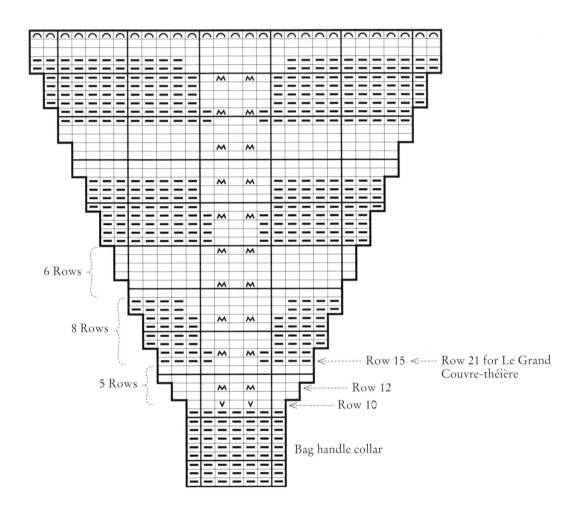

6 Rows

8 Rows

5 Rows

Row 15 ⟵------ Row 21 for Le Grand
Couvre-théière

Row 12

Row 10

Bag handle collar

LEGEND

☐	Knit on right side, Purl on wrong side
▬	Purl on right side, Knit on wrong side
v	Increase by knitting into the front and back of the stitch
ʍ	Make one (see page 15)
∩	Cast off

Abbreviations and terms

Knitting abbreviations and explanations

K = knit
P = purl
st/s = stitch/es
tog = together
mm = millimetre/s
in = inch/es
RS = right side
WS = wrong side
MC = main colour
CC = contrasting colour
garter st = garter stitch (knit every row)
st st = stocking stitch (1 row knit, 1 row purl)
M1 = make 1 (see page 15)

ssk = slip slip knit (slip 1 stitch knitwise, slip a second stitch knitwise, then insert the left needle through the front of both slipped stitches from left to right and knit them together. This method of decreasing makes the stitches slant to the left.)

K2tog = knit two together. This method of decreasing makes the stitches slant to the right.

Increase once in next stitch = knit (or purl, if you are on a purl row) into the front and back of the next stitch.

yo = yarn over (take the yarn over the needle before working the next stitch)

Crochet abbreviations and terms

ABBREV	AUSTRALIA/NZ/UK	ABBREV	US
ch	chain	ch	chain
sl st	slip stitch	slip st	slip stitch
dc	double crochet	sc	single crochet
htr	half treble	hdc	half double crochet
tr	treble	dc	double crochet
dtr	double treble	tr trc	treble triple crochet
triptr	triple treble	dtr dtrc	double treble double triple crochet
quadtr	quadruple treble	trip tr tr trc	triple treble triple triple crochet

Yarns – guidelines only

AUSTRALIA/UK	US	TENSION/GAUGE
3-ply, 4-ply, 5-ply, jumper weight	fingering	32–26 sts to 10 cm (4 in)
8-ply, dk, double knit	sport weight — double knit, light worsted	22–24 sts to 10 cm (4 in)

Stockists

Nundle Woollen Mill

1 Oakenville Street
Nundle NSW Australia 2340
1300 666 712 or 02 6769 3330
woollenmill@nundle.com
www.nundle.com

Wool Addiction

Shop 3, 20 Station Street
Bowral NSW Australia 2576
02 48 624799
info@wooladdiction.com.au
www.wooladdiction.com.au

Tangled Yarns

Studio A/9 Chester Street
Newstead QLD Australia 4006
07 3666 0276
tangled@tangledyarns.com.au
www.tangledyarns.com.au

Mosman Needlecraft

Shop 3, 529 Military Road
Mosman NSW Australia 2088
02 9969 5105
mosmanneedlecraft@bigpond.com
www.mosmanneedlecraft.com.au

Threads and More

Shop 7, 637 Sherwood Road
Sherwood, Brisbane Australia 4075
07 3379 6699
shop@threadsandmore.com.au
www.threadsandmore.com.au

Jo Sharp Hand Knitting Yarns

P.O. Box 357
Albany WA Australia 6331
0434 678 668
knitstore@bigpond.com
www.josharp.com

Wool Baa

124 Bridport Street
Albert Park Victoria Australia 3206
03 9690 6633
sales@woolbaa.com.au
www.woolbaa.com.au

Acknowledgements

I was chatting to my boy Ben yesterday. (At the time of writing, this book is in design/layout stage.) Ben is hardly a boy at twenty-six, but he will always be MY boy. Anyway, I was chatting to Ben about the book and he asked if there was a cosy dedicated to him. He was a bit miffed that there wasn't, but I reminded him he already had a whole book dedicated to him. *Really Wild Tea Cosies* — for my mother, Kate, who would have smiled so wide and for my son, Benjamin, who makes me smile so wide.

Frankly I was a bit chuffed that he was a bit miffed. It speaks tomes about a young man who wants to have a tea cosy dedicated all to himself, don't you think?

THE SON

I'm very proud of you too Ben.

THE BLOKE

I must have done something good in a past life to get my fella. Hey you, Julian Pepperell. Love ya darls. Still. For good. What would I do without you?

DIANA HILL

One of the fun things you get to do when you have a book is to start sentences with 'My Publisher'. Saying 'My Publisher' in the middle of a sentence is pretty cool too. But sometimes when an author says 'My Publisher' they are talking about a singular person, not a corporation. My (singular person) Publisher is Diana Hill. What a woman! We haven't always agreed along the way but I have always trusted and respected her final decisions. She has taken the best care of me and of my books, *Really Wild Tea Cosies* and *How Tea Cosies Changed the World*. Thank you Diana, for your finely tuned skills, your naughty humour and your very good will.

THE MIGHTY MURDOCH MICE

Making a book is like making a movie. So roll the credits all you good people. I can't imagine I'm an EASY author to play with but still you make me want to come back for more. Senior Editor, Sophia Oravecz — oh how you have stayed calm and professional. Designer, Emma Gough — oh what a beautiful book. Photographer, Jared Fowler and Stylist, Emma Ross — oh how you made my cosies shine. Thank you.

THE EDITOR (AKA STEELY)

Georgina Bitcon is an author's nightmare. And a dream. She has a mind like a steel trap. Nothing, and I mean NOTHING, gets past her. Praise the heavens for Steely. Errrrr — Georgina.

THREE FABULOUS KNITTERS

I had test knitters, yes I did. Three test knitters. Maree of Orange, Kerrie of Quorrobolong (near Newcastle) and Mrs Olix Dax. Thank you, you fabulous women.

Published in 2012 by Murdoch Books Pty Limited

Murdoch Books Australia
Pier 8/9
23 Hickson Road
Millers Point NSW 2000
Phone: +61 (0) 2 8220 2000
Fax: +61 (0) 2 8220 2558
www.murdochbooks.com.au
info@murdochbooks.com.au

Murdoch Books UK Limited
Erico House, 6th Floor
93–99 Upper Richmond Road
Putney, London SW15 2TG
Phone: +44 (0) 20 8785 5995
Fax: +44 (0) 20 8785 5985
www.murdochbooks.co.uk
info@murdochbooks.co.uk

For Corporate Orders & Custom Publishing contact Noel Hammond,
National Business Development Manager Murdoch Books Australia

Publisher: Diana Hill
Designer: Emma Gough
Photographer: Jared Fowler
Stylist: Emma Ross
Editor: Georgina Bitcon
Production: Joan Beal

National Library of Australia Cataloguing-in-Publication entry

Prior, Loani.
How tea cosies changed the world / Loani Prior.
9781742664002 (pbk.)
Tea cozies.
Knitting—Patterns.
Crocheting—Patterns.

746.43041

A catalogue record for this book is available from the British Library.

Printed by 1010 Printing International Limited, China